# Passport's Illustrated Guide to

# NEW ZEALAND

### THIRD EDITION

S0-BOL-887

**FROM**
**THOMAS COOK**

## PASSPORT BOOKS
*NTC/Contemporary Publishing Group*

Published by Passport Books,
a division of NTC/Contemporary Publishing Group, Inc.
4255 West Touhy Avenue,
Lincolnwood (Chicago), Illinois
60646–1975 U.S.A.

**Written by** Nick Hanna

**Original photography by** Paul Kenward

Edited, designed, and produced by AA Publishing.
© The Automobile Association 1996, 1999.
Maps © The Automobile Association 1996, 1999.

Library of Congress Catalog Card Number: 99-74063

ISBN 0-8442-1179-6

The contents of this publication are believed correct at the time of
printing. Nevertheless, the publishers cannot accept responsibility for
any errors or omissions, or for changes in the details given in this guide,
or for the consequences of any reliance on the information provided by
the same. Assessments of attractions, hotels, restaurants, and so forth
are based upon the author's own experience and therefore descriptions
given in this guide necessarily contain an element of subjective opinion
which may not reflect the publisher's opinion or dictate a reader's own
experiences on another occasion.
**We have tried to ensure accuracy in this guide, but things do
change and we would be grateful if readers would advise us of any
inaccuracies they may encounter.**

Published by Passport Books in conjunction with AA Publishing and the
Thomas Cook Group Ltd.

Color separation: BTB Colour Reproduction, Whitchurch, Hampshire,
England.

Printed by Edicoes ASA, Oporto, Portugal.

Cover photographs: front, AA Photo Library; spine, Corbis Digital
Stock.

# Contents

BACKGROUND —————— 5

   Introduction 6
   Geography 8
   Flora 12
   Fauna 14
   History 16
   Culture 18
   Politics 20
   Ecotourism in the Year 2000 22

FIRST STEPS —————— 23

WHAT TO SEE —————— 29

   Auckland and Northland 30
   Central North Island 52
   Wellington and Taranaki 76
   Nelson and Marlborough 90
   Central South Island 102
   The Deep South 126

GETTING AWAY FROM IT ALL 145

DIRECTORY —————— 151

   Shopping 152
   Entertainment 156
   Children 160
   Sport 162
   Food and Drink 166
   Hotels and Accommodation 172
   On Business 176
   Practical Guide 178

INDEX AND
ACKNOWLEDGEMENTS —————— 190

## Maps

Locator 6
New Zealand 7
Auckland and Northland 30–1
Auckland Environs 36–7
Devonport walk 42
Central North Island 52–3
Coromandel tour 74
Wellington and Taranaki 77
Wellington 83
Nelson and Marlborough 90–1
Kaikoura Peninsula Walkway 100
Central South Island 102–3
Christchurch 104–5
Banks Peninsula tour 120
Hooker Valley walk 122
TranzAlpine Express tour 124
The Deep South 126–7
Otago Peninsula tour 138
Milford Sound tour 140
The Routeburn Track 142

## Features

Hot Lakes and Volcanoes 10
Historic Houses 38
Early Explorers 50
Maori Society 68
Sheep 110
Maori Arts, Crafts and Dance 158

## Walks and Tours

Devonport walk 42
Coromandel tour 74
Wellington walk 88
Kaikoura Peninsula Walkway 100
Banks Peninsula tour 120

Hooker Valley walk 122
TranzAlpine Express tour 124
Otago Peninsula tour 138
Milford Sound tour 140
The Routeburn Track 142

# About this Book

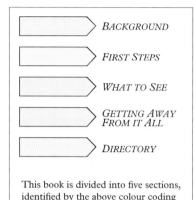

BACKGROUND

FIRST STEPS

WHAT TO SEE

GETTING AWAY
FROM IT ALL

DIRECTORY

This book is divided into five sections,
identified by the above colour coding

Thermal landscapes are just one of the
attractions in this diverse country

The **Background** gives an introduction
to the country – its history, geography,
politics, culture.
**First Steps** offers practical advice on
arriving and getting around.
**What to See** is an alphabetical listing of
places to visit, divided into six regions,
interspersed with walks and tours.
**Getting Away From it All** highlights
places off the beaten track where it's
possible to relax and enjoy peace and
quiet.
Finally the **Directory** provides practical
information – from shopping and
entertainment to children and sport,
including a section on business matters.
Special highly illustrated features on
specific aspects of the country appear
throughout the book.

# BACKGROUND

'*Whatu ngarongaro he tangata,
toitu he whenua.*'
'Man perishes but the land
remains.'
**MAORI PROVERB**

# Introduction

*A*lthough a little further flung than most other travel destinations, New Zealand abundantly repays the effort it takes to get there – as many people are discovering. This beautiful country is now placed firmly on the world tourism map.

## LOCATOR

Extending just 1,755km from north to south, New Zealand has everything you could possibly want for a refreshing and completely different type of holiday.

One of the country's most obvious attractions is the appeal of the great outdoors, and in this respect you won't be disappointed: this clean, unpolluted land has 13 national parks, which between them cover nearly 30 per cent of the nation. These parks encompass lakes and rivers swarming with trout, stunning fiords and glaciers, mighty volcanoes and bubbling geysers, golden beaches and bays, and mountains and hills with fern-filled, mossy gorges and tumbling waterfalls hidden away on their forested slopes. There are no native land mammals, but instead New Zealand has a range of rare and extraordinary birds. Meanwhile, marine mammals such as whales, dolphins and seals flourish in the surrounding seas.

This is the image of New Zealand we know, but less well publicised is a new-found intellectual and cultural confidence which is manifested in literature, film, painting and sculpture, handicrafts, performing arts and even fashion design. Creativity has added a cosmopolitan air to many towns and cities, building on the unique blend of Maori and European cultures which is New Zealand's own. Alongside this cultural outpouring, New Zealand cuisine has also shrugged off its boring image and developed a distinctive style which complements the nation's now

### Thomas Cook's New Zealand

*Thomas Cook first included New Zealand in its Australasia tours in 1880, hailing it as 'the South Pacific Wonderland ... undoubtedly the grandest country in the world for the tourist, being so remarkable for wild landscape beauty'.*
*The following year the company offered excursions from Auckland to the 'Hot Lakes' of the North Island ('ten days for Twelve Pounds, inclusive of all charges'), and the first Thomas Cook office opened in the capital in 1889. Today, Thomas Cook has branches throughout the country.*

# NEW ZEALAND

internationally famous wines. Those who thought New Zealand was still an unsophisticated backwater are in for a big surprise.

An excellent tourist infrastructure and the relaxed, welcoming attitude of the New Zealanders add considerably to the enjoyment of this uncrowded country, christened Aotearoa, or 'Land of the Long White Cloud', by Maori.

# Geography

*N*ew Zealand lies almost exactly half-way between the Equator and the South Pole and is divided into two main islands (the North Island and the South Island), a third, smaller island (Stewart Island, off the southern tip of the South Island), and a scattering of little islands to the south and east of the main land masses.

## The land

The landscapes of New Zealand are dominated by the ranges of mountains and hills that run through both islands; there are 223 named peaks of more than 2,300m, the highest being Mount Cook in the South Island, and over 75 per cent of the country lies more than 200m above sea-level. This rugged topography has given rise to a huge variety of land forms and ecological zones, the only temperate-zone habitat not found here being true desert.

The two main islands are relatively narrow, so no inland location lies more than 110km from the sea as the crow flies.

This forest near Taupo is just one of numerous timber plantations throughout the country

## Climate

New Zealand has an oceanic temperate climate and, due to its isolation from other land masses, seasonal variations are relatively minimal. The seasons are the reverse of those in the northern hemisphere (see **Climate** on page 180). The country's North Island is generally warmer than the South Island.

## Population

New Zealand's total population is around 3.6 million, with almost 75 per cent (2.73 million) living in the North Island. Just under a quarter of the entire population (over 991,800 people) live in the greater Auckland area.

Around 79.5 per cent of New Zealanders are European in origin, mostly of English or Scottish descent, with a handful of Irish or Welsh ancestry and a significant number from Holland. Approximately 13 per cent of the population is Maori and 5 per cent Polynesians from the South Pacific islands (such as Samoa, Tonga and the Cook Islands), who are mostly concentrated in Auckland. Recently, immigration has been increasing from Asian countries such as Vietnam, Laos, Cambodia, Hong Kong and Taiwan.

## The economy

Despite the lack of flat ground, agriculture and horticulture dominate the economy and account for 60 per cent

Cleared of forest in the last century, rolling farmlands now support millions of sheep

of export earnings (see also **Sheep** on pages 110–11).

The country has some of the world's largest man-made forests, growing timber (mostly the versatile radiata pine, introduced from California) for use in pulp and paper mills and for lumber. With a worldwide decrease in the amount of timber available, and the fact that much of New Zealand's 1.2 million hectares of planted forests are now reaching maturity, the country is expected to profit from this resource well into the next century.

Commercial fishing is also an important export earner, with an annual quota system ensuring the sustainable management of fish species within the country's 320km EEZ (Exclusive Economic Zone). Aquaculture (fish farming) is also on the increase as there are many ideal sites in the hundreds of sheltered bays and inlets around the country's 15,000km coastline.

The increasing popularity of New Zealand's high-quality wines has also meant a boom in demand for the country's winemakers (see page 168).

Tourism is a crucial component in the economy, with just over 1.5 million annual visitors generating an estimated NZ$4.8 billion in foreign exchange and supporting 74,000 full-time jobs. Tourism is growing at nearly three times the average rate for world tourism. A strategic plan for the expansion of tourism envisages 3 million annual arrivals by the year 2000, generating an estimated NZ$9 billion in foreign exchange.

# HOT LAKES

The earth's crust is made up of moving plates up to 60km thick. New Zealand marks the boundary of two plates that are moving together and forms the southern extremity of the Pacific 'Ring of Fire'. At the North Island one plate is being forced under another (subducted), melting to produce magma that is extruded through volcanoes. Underground water that meets this molten rock becomes superheated, returning to the surface as hot lakes or geysers. At the South Island meanwhile, the plates are forcing one another up, and here are produced the mighty peaks of the Southern Alps.

Volcanic activity is largely responsible for shaping the surface of New Zealand, creating some of its most dramatic mountains and lakes. The city of Auckland stands on a series of 50 or more extinct volcanoes, while much of the central North Island was built up into a volcanic plateau by successive eruptions in the distant past.

A fault line runs down the North Island; at its centre is Rotorua, the

# AND VOLCANOES

Volcanic activity is harnessed to provide energy at Ohaaki (top left) and Wairakei (inset) geothermal power stations

country's most famous thermal zone, and at its end is White Island, an active volcano 50km off shore in the Bay of Plenty. To the south of Rotorua is the country's largest lake, Taupo, which was shaped by violent explosions that began some 250,000 years ago; in the most recent eruption (AD 185) over 150cu km of pumice and ash were ejected over vast areas of the North Island. But even this is dwarfed by an eruption that took place some 22,600 years ago (dubbed Kawakawa by geologists), which new data shows was the largest eruption to have taken place in the world during the last 50,000 years.

Maori made use of the region's geothermal power, often siting their villages on active thermal fields which provided heating in winter and boiling pools for cooking. Today, the energy is still used, the geothermal power stations at Wairakei (near Lake Taupo) and nearby Ohaaki generating 7 per cent of the country's energy needs.

# Flora

*A*s a result of New Zealand's isolation from other land masses for millenia, numerous unique species of plants have evolved, many of which survive today despite the effects of over 1,000 years of human settlement. No less than 2,500 plant species are endemic, as are 1,450 of the 1,650 flowering plants found

### Forest types

Although only a quarter of the original forests (which once covered 80 per cent of the country) remain today, most of these are protected as national parks, forest parks and reserves. The majority of indigenous trees are evergreens, with only a handful of deciduous species.

In the North Island, the forests are

mostly tropical or subtropical in nature, with a dense canopy and an understorey of almost impenetrable shrubs and tree ferns. Climbers and epiphytes (such as orchids) flourish in these moisture-laden hothouses. In the South Island the forests show traces of sub-Antarctic origin, characterised by several species of beech, and with a more open forest floor.

### The trees

Of particular note are the giant conifers, such as the *kauri*; the king of the forests, this magnificent tree can reach heights of up to 60m and may take 1,500 years to reach full maturity. The first 20m or so of its massive, silvery grey trunk soar upwards as a clean shaft, unblemished by any branches – the fact that the *kauri* was perfect for ships' masts was soon recognised by early colonists, and the straight-grained, unknotted wood was highly prized in the 19th century. As a result, most of the original 3 million hectares of *kauri* in the North Island were felled by 1860; just 10,000 hectares remain standing today.

Other conifers include the *rimu*, which, like the *kauri*, has a straight, branchless trunk and was an important timber tree. Maori made considerable use of the *totara*, which is easily carved and handy for building canoes and houses; found all over New Zealand, this

This massive *kauri* in the North Island, Tane Mahuta, is thought to be 2,000 years old

Tree ferns are just one of 150 species of ferns which thrive in New Zealand

species can grow to a height of up to 30m. Man-made forest plantations are dominated by the *radiata* or Monterey pine, Douglas fir and redwoods.

The most notable of the many flowering trees in New Zealand is the beautiful *pohutukawa*, which grows largely around the North Island coast and flames into scarlet blossom in December – hence its nickname, the 'New Zealand Christmas tree'. Equally attractive are the rich red flowers of the *rata*, the golden-yellow *kowhai* and the snowy-white ribbonwoods.

New Zealand has only one true palm, the *nikau* palm, which is the world's most southerly growing palm. The cabbage tree looks very much like a palm and adds a tropical air to landscapes everywhere, although in fact it is the largest member of the lily family.

There are also over 150 different species of fern (plus numerous hybrids), ranging from tiny ferns which only unfold on rainy days to giant tree ferns over 15m high.

### Alpine plants

Above the forest line, scrub and tussock give way to rolling meadows which are ablaze with alpines during the summer. Gentians, eyebrights, forget-me-nots, giant edelweiss and mountain daisies grow in profusion. Also found here is the world's largest buttercup, the Mount Cook lily, and the largest forget-me-not in the world, the Chatham Island lily.

### Cushion plants

One of the most curious plants in New Zealand is the vegetable sheep, which grows in low mounds and is covered in cream-coloured, woolly-looking leaves – hence the name, since from a distance it looks like a resting sheep! Another of the so-called cushion plants is the giant vegetable sheep, which only grows in the highlands around Nelson.

Crimson blossoms on the *pohutukawa* tree

# Fauna

*I*t is clear that New Zealand must have split away from the ancient continent of Gondwanaland (present-day Australia, Antarctic, India, Africa and South America) before the appearance of mammals, since none (apart from three species of bat) are endemic to the country. Instead, many unique flightless birds filled the ecological niches elsewhere occupied by mammals, the absence of predators making the country a paradise for them.

## Extinct species

But this paradise was not to last: the first Maori settlers brought rats and the Maori dog (now extinct), and Europeans introduced over 50 species of animals – Captain Cook freed the first sheep, soon followed by pigs, cows, deer, rabbits, cats and possums. Combined with the loss of forest habitat through clearance for agriculture, the effect on birdlife was devastating: 41 species are now extinct, and 57 species remain threatened despite breeding and conservation programmes.

Among the more spectacular losses were those of the moas (of which there were once 25 different species, including the largest bird ever to walk on earth, *Dinornis maximus*, standing 4m tall) and the New Zealand eagle, the largest eagle ever known, with talons the size of a tiger's claws.

The kiwi is now an endangered species due to predation by stoats, possums and dogs

## Flightless birds

New Zealand's national bird, the kiwi, is the best-known flightless bird. There are three species of kiwi – brown, great spotted and little spotted – all similar in appearance, with vestigial wings, strong legs, and nostrils on the end of a long, flexible beak. Kiwis are nocturnal, and may have evolved thus to avoid being preyed upon by the giant eagles; today stoats, possums and dogs are their greatest enemies. Population estimates are vague, but earlier optimism has been dispelled and kiwis are now classified as endangered.

More easily visible is the cheeky weka, a mischievous member of the rail family often seen strutting around campsites stealing food or shiny objects. You are highly unlikely to see the brilliantly hued takahe in the wild; once thought to be extinct, a small colony of these birds was discovered in Fiordland in 1948, but the total population still numbers only around 150.

## Other birdlife

Other native species include the kaka, a forest parrot, and its cousin the kea, which is renowned for its vandalous habits – hikers have found their boots and even tents pecked to pieces by this fearless and intelligent bird. The unusual kakapo has long, hair-like feathers growing from the base of its bill, which it uses to find its way around at night; only 48 individuals of this highly endangered species are known to exist.

In rural areas you might well hear a small native owl, the morepork, whose cry gave rise to its common name. The melodious songs of both the tui and the bellbird can be heard on forest walks. The large and strikingly coloured native pigeon is found over most of the country and feeds on shoots and berries.

New Zealand's black stilt, or kaki, is the world's rarest wading bird. These slender, red-legged birds were once widespread, but there are now only a few left in the wild. The white-bodied pied stilt is, however, common and can be found throughout wetland areas.

## Reptiles

Amongst a range of small reptiles that are native to New Zealand is the extraordinary tuatara, which has the longest unbroken ancestry of any living animal and whose predecessors date back to the Triassic period, some 200 million years ago. Often erroneously referred to as a lizard, the tuatara can grow up to 60cm in length and has a ridge of spines along its back. These nocturnal animals live on a number of isolated, offshore islands and are fully protected.

The tuatara is an ancient reptile which can grow up to 60cm in length

# History

**AD 950**

The Polynesian explorer Kupe discovers New Zealand, which he names Aotearoa ('Land of the Long White Cloud').

**1350**

Overpopulation in their home islands forces many Polynesians to set sail for Aotearoa in a fleet of large canoes.

**1642**

The Dutch explorer Abel Janszoon Tasman sights land at Hokitika on 13 December; he later anchors in Golden Bay but never goes ashore.

**1769**

Captain James Cook arrives on board the *Endeavour* on 9 October at Gisborne. On this and subsequent voyages he plots the coastline.

**1790**

Sealers, whalers and timber traders arrive. Maori exchange their traditional war clubs for firearms and inter-tribal wars take on a new, bloodier dimension.

**1814**

The Reverend Samuel Marsden under the aegis of the Anglican Church Mission Society sets up the first mission station, gradually making converts and trying to halt cannibalism. The first settlers arrive.

**1817**

The excesses of the more lawless settlers provoke the British to extend New South Wales legislation to New Zealand.

**1832**

The first British resident, James Busby, arrives from Australia, but his efforts to promote law and order and to protect the Maori are ineffective. Pressure grows for the British to assume full authority.

**1839**

Captain William Hobson is sent from London and appointed Lieutenant Governor with the intention of persuading Maori chiefs to relinquish their sovereignty to the British Crown.

**1840**

Hobson negotiates the Treaty of Waitangi, which is signed by more than 45 chiefs on 6 February outside his residence at Waitangi in the Bay of Islands. The treaty is later taken around the country, and another 500 chiefs sign. Although the treaty claimed to guarantee the Maori possession in perpetuity of their lands, forests and fisheries, its provisions have always been a source of dispute.

**1840–8**

Numerous organised settlements are established, notably Wellington, Wanganui, Nelson, New Plymouth, Christchurch and Dunedin.

**1843**

The first skirmishes in what is to become the bloody and protracted Land Wars, as Maori resist what they see as the illegal seizure of their tribal territories.

**1852**

The first gold strikes are made, and gold rushes bring in thousands of prospectors to Coromandel, Otago and Westland. The first large-scale sheep stations are established.

**1860**

The Land Wars escalate, with armed conflict lasting for almost two decades in the North Island. The Maori display impressive military tactics and relentless bravery, but are eventually overwhelmed by the better-equipped colonial armies. To punish the Maori, vast areas of land are confiscated.

**1865**

The capital is moved from Auckland to Wellington.

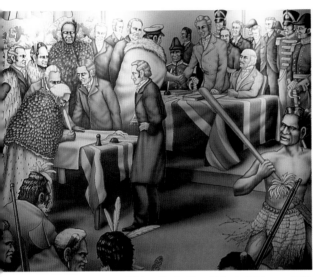

The signing of the Treaty of Waitangi in the Bay of Islands, 6 February, 1840

**1973**
Britain joins the EEC (now the European Union), and New Zealand is left to seek a new economic role for itself as preferential trading links with Britain end.

**1984**
The Labour Party is elected, initiating a nuclear-free policy and provoking the USA to exclude the country from the regional ANZUS defence pact. Free-market policies are introduced, signalling a decade of radical change.

**1867**
Maori gain the vote, and the first four Maori members are elected to Parliament.

**1882**
The first refrigerated ship sails to Europe with a cargo of frozen meat, signalling the beginning of a new economic era as sheep farming becomes the lifeblood of the country.

**1893**
New Zealand becomes the first sovereign state to introduce votes for women, one of many reforms towards the end of the century which put it at the forefront of social change.

**1907**
New Zealand becomes an autonomous dominion within the British Empire.

**1947**
New Zealand becomes an independent, autonomous member of the British Commonwealth of Nations.

**1990**
The National Party ousts Labour, but continues with deregulation.

**1993**
New Zealanders vote in a referendum in favour of Mixed Member Proportional (MMP) representation.

**1994**
The idea that New Zealand should become a republic is first floated, but is quashed by the Prime Minister.

**1996**
First Mixed Member Proportional (MMP) representational election held. Maori-dominated New Zealand First hold balance of power, and following political manoeuvring, New Zealand gains its first female prime minister.

**2000**
New Zealand hosts the America's Cup.

# Culture

*W*hether they arrived by canoe, boat or aeroplane, all New Zealanders can trace their ancestry to immigrant stock, the legacy of which is a strongly pragmatic streak in the nation's character. Ingenuity and a 'let's fix it' attitude apply as much to topical political issues as to broken-down farm machinery, and these traits – combined with an innate sense of fairness and a strong sense of principle – are an integral part of the national identity.

### Just beer, rugby and racing?

The popular image of New Zealanders is that their interests focus around just three things – beer, rugby and racing. The first needs no explanation, and as for the second it would perhaps be more accurate to say simply that New Zealanders love sport, for although the country's national rugby team, the All Blacks, has a devoted following, so do many other sports – from aerobics to yachting. Horse-racing is a particular passion, and many towns and communities have a racetrack just outside town.

While there is a great deal of truth in this image, it also belies a cultural sophistication which is less well known. Despite the country's small population, music and live theatre flourish. There is also a strong strand of talent in opera – New Zealand opera singers include the late Oscar Natzke and Inia Te Wiata (both basses), as well as Sir Donald McIntyre, Dame

Malvina Major and Dame Kiri Te Kanawa, to name only the best known.

New Zealand's artists embrace styles as diverse as those of Colin McCahon, a pioneer modernist, and Ralph Hotere, who draws on Maori and Pacific Island motifs for inspiration. Contemporary Maori art – particularly carving – has become a significant movement.

Perhaps the best-known New Zealand writer was Katherine Mansfield, but a new generation has now risen to international prominence, starting with Keri Hulme, whose novel *The Bone People* marked a fresh strand in Maori writing which continues today through authors such as Patricia Grace and Witi Ihimaera. The film industry is also thriving, with Jane Campion's Oscar-winning *The Piano* followed soon after by the release in 1994 of the ground-breaking *Once Were Warriors*, a raw, violent story

Dame Kiri Te Kanawa, an international star

The All Blacks national rugby team perform a fearsome 'haka' before every match

about contemporary urban Maori life based on Alan Duff's powerful book.

## The Kiwis

As well as being the name for the national bird, the word kiwi is widely used to describe New Zealanders themselves. In the money markets it is also a nickname for the New Zealand dollar, and Americans use it as an abbreviation for kiwifruit (although no Kiwi would use it in this way).

*Pakeha* is the Maori word for a Kiwi of European descent, although you are more likely to see this in print than hear it in speech – unless talking with a Maori. Interestingly, Maori had no collective name for themselves before the coming of the Europeans, and it was only later on that they used the word *maori* to refer to themselves – in their language, it means 'usual' or 'normal'.

The New Zealanders' capacity for understatement is legendary and they are often self-deprecating when it comes to their own achievements – except when they beat their nearest neighbours, Australia, on the rugby or cricket field. 'Oz' is generally regarded with friendly rivalry and derision, and in much the same way people in the South Island (to which they refer jokingly as 'the mainland') complain that North Islanders ignore them politically and – almost as bad – prefer to go overseas for their holidays rather than visit them.

# Politics

$N$ew Zealand is a sovereign state with a democratic government based on the British parliamentary system (except that there is no Upper House). The legislative body, the House of Representatives, comprising 19 members, is elected for a three-year term. The Queen is the titular head of state, represented in New Zealand by a Governor-General.

### The Muldoon muddle

Post-war politics in New Zealand was dominated by the National Party and, in particular, by its now-discredited leader Sir Robert Muldoon. His highly interventionist regime controlled everything from subsidies to prices and pay, almost bankrupting an economy which was at the same time reeling from rising oil prices and the loss of protected markets when Britain joined the EEC.

### Radical reforms

In 1984 Muldoon was thrown out, to be replaced by a Labour Party (led by the charismatic David Lange) intent on sweeping reforms that included privatisation, deregulation and the removal of subsidies.

This experiment in free-market economics, focused principally on agriculture and industry, was successful in reducing the government deficit by the end of the 1980s, but the electorate balked at the high cost (principally an

The 'Beehive' parliament building, Wellington

Dame Whina Cooper was an active campaigner for Maori rights until her death in 1994

unemployment rate of over 9 per cent) and in 1990 Labour lost power to the National Party under the Right Honourable (Jim) James Brendan Bolger.

Stealing their rivals' ideological clothes, the National Party took the axe to the labour and financial markets and government spending. New Zealand is now reaping the benefits of these reforms, with falling inflation and a growth rate that continues to exceed predictions.

## Constitutional changes

In 1993, a plebiscite was held on constitutional change and the electorate voted to adopt MMP (Mixed Member Proportional) representation, a system which aims to give smaller parties a say in parliament. The first MMP elections were held in 1996, with National and Labour sharing the majority of the vote, but the balance of power being retained by the newly formed New Zealand First, a Maori-dominated party. The Maori voice is now being heard in parliament as never before.

## Land rights

The issue of land rights has dominated Maori politics since the Land Wars of the last century. The problem originated with the Treaty of Waitangi in 1840, which comprised two texts, one in English and one in Maori, each differing significantly in the translation. Whereas in the English text Maori ceded 'sovereignty', in the Maori text they gave the British the right of governance. The wordings also differ on the issue of land ownership.

A century and a half of frustration and anger over the alienation of Maori from their land came to a head when Maori civil rights campaigner, Whina Cooper, then 80 years old, captured the public imagination with her 'great march' on Parliament in 1975, drawing 5,000 supporters along the 1,100km route. Later made a Dame, she was the most influential Maori woman of the century and came to be known as 'the Mother of the Nation'; she died in 1994.

The Waitangi Tribunal was set up in the same year, and since then has been the official forum for resolving grievances. Although many claims have since been settled, disputes simmer on – to the detriment of race relations and future stability.

In 1994, the government proposed an all-embracing settlement which would encompass all land seized, stolen or taken by unfair means throughout the country; the potential costs to the Crown could amount to as much as NZ$1 billion over the next 10 years. Whether this 'final settlement' will prove acceptable to Maori or even affordable for the Crown remains to be seen.

# Ecotourism in the Year 2000

New Zealand's 'clean, green' image draws many thousands of visitors to the country, and yet the very presence of tourists may be threatening fragile areas as it has done in many other parts of the world. With tourism arrivals projected to increase to 2 or 3 million per annum by the year 2000, can the environment withstand the impact?

The natural environment is well protected by law

develops on a sustainable basis. The tourism industry has produced its own 'Code of Environmental Principles', and most operators are aware that their resource base (nature itself) is their most important asset. The Department of Conservation, which manages nearly 30 per cent of the country's land area in national parks, forests and reserves, is one of the most successful in the world.

Already some major natural attractions (such as the Waitomo Caves, Mount Cook National Park, and the Fox and Franz Josef glaciers) are close to their capacity at peak times of year, their facilities rapidly becoming inadequate to cope with visitor numbers. Many of the more popular three- to five-day walking tracks are also becoming overcrowded, with insufficient spaces in overnight huts. Milford Sound has become almost as busy as the Grand Canyon, with a constant procession of 'flightseeing' aeroplanes and helicopters drowning out the commentaries on the boats below.

Fortunately, many of these problems have been identified and strategies defined which will ensure that tourism

Most importantly, New Zealand took a significant step in the right direction with the introduction in 1991 of the Resource Management Act, which enshrined in law the sustainable management of the environment (including the nation's cultural and historic heritage). This landmark legislation has been hailed as the leading edge of environmental planning, and other countries (including the USA) are now looking to New Zealand in an attempt to emulate its policies for tourism and nature conservation. It seems that here, at least, is one country where ecotourism may turn out to be more than just an empty buzzword.

# FIRST STEPS

'The day was the perfection
of New Zealand weather,
which is the perfection of all
climates – hot, but rarely
sultry, bright, but not
glaring, from the vivid green
with which the earth is
generally clothed.'
**BISHOP SELWYN,**
*Journal letter, 1843*

# First Steps

## PLANNING YOUR ITINERARY

New Zealand has such an incredible range of action-packed attractions that deciding where to go and what to see can seem daunting. However, it is a fairly compact country and you can do an enormous amount in a relatively short space of time if you set your mind to it. But because many activities are weather-dependent, it is best not to structure your trip too tightly – a flexible itinerary will allow you to make the most of the endless repertoire of things to do. A hit list of the best New Zealand has to offer might include the following:

**Aerial sightseeing** – ballooning (Christchurch), ski-plane landings (Mount Cook), helicopter flights (Mount Tarawera from Rotorua, Fox and Franz Josef glaciers, Mount Cook).

**Beaches** – Bay of Islands, Bay of Plenty, East Cape, Coromandel, Waiheke Island, Abel Tasman National Park.

**Bird-watching** – Cape Kidnappers, Farewell Spit, Hauraki Gulf, Mount Bruce National Wildlife Reserve, Paparoa National Park, Stewart Island, Taiaroa Head (Otago Peninsula).

**Cruising** – Hauraki Gulf, Bay of Islands, Marlborough Sounds, Fiordland.

**Dramatic scenery** – almost everywhere, but particularly the Mount Cook National Park, Fox and Franz Josef glaciers and Fiordland.

**Museums** – Auckland Museum, Hobson Wharf Maritime Museum, Kelly

Touring by coach is one way to appreciate the scenic splendours of New Zealand

Floatplanes are just one option for aerial sightseeing

Tarlton's Underwater World and Antarctic Encounter (Auckland); Museum of New Zealand, Katherine Mansfield Birthplace (Wellington); International Antarctic Centre and Canterbury Museum (Christchurch), Otago and Settlers Museum (Dunedin).

**Thrills and spills** – black-water rafting (Waitomo), jet-boating and white-water rafting (almost everywhere), bungee-jumping (Queenstown and Lake Taupo).

**Wildlife** – swimming with dolphins (Bay of Islands and Whakatane), whale-watching (Kaikoura), seal- and penguin-watching (Otago Peninsula).

**Volcanic activity** – Rotorua, Tongariro National Park, White Island.

## GETTING AROUND

Despite the wild, rugged nature of much of New Zealand, the country has a well-developed transport system and the distances between places of interest or activities aren't overwhelming. Travelling around, whether by public transport or by car, is quick and easy.

### By air

Air New Zealand, Ansett New Zealand and Mt Cook Airlines provide scheduled services between major cities, towns and resorts.

### By rail

New Zealand Rail provides several different InterCity rail services. One of the most popular rail routes for visitors is the TranzAlpine Express (see pages 124–5).

### By coach

There is an extensive network of coach services linking most towns and cities. Several companies offer 'alternative' coach services, particularly popular with young travellers, which provide stops at places of interest and a casual, friendly atmosphere; this is a great way to meet people as well as get to know the country. Bus and coach services within towns and cities are also good.

### By car

The flexibility and independence which a rental car provides makes it by far the most attractive option for touring New Zealand. For short periods rental cars are fairly expensive, but generous discounts can often be negotiated for longer-term rentals of a month or more. A car and tent is a good combination, or alternatively consider hiring a campervan if you are travelling with your family.

Despite an extensive network of sealed (tarmacked) roads, some back-country roads are still unsealed and there may be restrictions for rental cars in some areas. On the whole, driving in New Zealand is a pleasure. There are, however, several Kiwi peculiarities (such as one-way, single-lane bridges on some main roads) of which you should be aware. See page 182 for more details on this and other aspects of internal travel.

A network of information centres provides friendly, helpful advice

## Information

One of the great things about travelling around New Zealand is the amount of detailed information which is available to help you make the most of your trip. Much of this is channelled through more than 80 information centres, co-ordinated by the New Zealand Tourism Board (NZTB), which form the Visitor Information Network. The centres' friendly, helpful staff provide impartial, up-to-date information on everything from bus travel to bungee-jumping.

A complementary service is offered by the Department of Conservation (DOC), which runs equally efficient and helpful visitor centres in national parks and at major natural attractions. The DOC visitor centres often incorporate high-quality displays on the local environment. The network of AA offices is also a source of information for visiting members and offers them reciprocal services.

## Meeting Kiwis

New Zealanders are renowned for their friendliness and hospitality, and have an outgoing, relaxed attitude towards visitors. Apart from the usual courtesies, there are no particular pitfalls to beware of – with the possible exception of comparing them unfavourably to Australians!

One of the best ways of meeting people and finding out more about the Kiwi way of life is to spend a few days in a homestay or farmstay (see page 174). These range from the cheap and cheerful to the highly sophisticated.

The *hongi*, a
Maori form of
greeting

**Maori etiquette**
All Maori tribes,
many sub-tribes
and community
groups, and even
universities and
schools still have
their *marae*
(courtyard – see
pages 68–9). The
protocol
governing *marae* is
highly formalised,
and it is very
important that
you seek
permission before
entering the *whare
runanga* (meeting-house) on any *marae*,
and walk around the *marae* rather than
across it; footwear must be removed
before going inside a *whare runanga*. It is
more than likely, however, that your visit
to a *marae* will be part of an organised
tour, in which case you will be told what
to do.

The Maori greeting *kia ora*, which
means both 'good health' and 'welcome',
is answered with the same words.

**Smoke-free zones**
New Zealand is a health-conscious
nation and smoking is on the decline
(it has the lowest rate of tobacco
consumption of any First World
country). Smoking is banned on all
public transport and in most public
places (such as government offices).
Many restaurants are also completely
non-smoking, although you can still light
up in bars and clubs.

**What to bring**
Almost any item you may require, from
camera film to contraceptives, is easily
obtainable in New Zealand, but the
relatively small market base and a Goods
and Service tax (GST) of 12.5 per cent
means that many goods are comparatively expensive.

It is also worth noting that the
weather can be highly variable from one
area to the next, and whereas one day
you might be comfortable in a T-shirt
and shorts, the next you might be better
off in a sou'wester! The best advice is to
come prepared for highly changeable
conditions.

In a country which is so geared
towards the outdoors, dress is casual,
but if you plan to sample any of the
more up-market restaurants in the cities
it is a good idea to pack some smart
clothes as many establishments set
minimum dress codes.

With the depletion of the ozone layer, covering up in the sun is increasingly important

## Sandflies and sunburn

New Zealand has neither dangerous animals nor snakes, but, as if to make up for this total lack of hazards, it does have the ubiquitous sandfly. These vicious insects were even noted by Captain Cook, who wrote in his journal on 11 May, 1773, at Dusky Sound that 'the most mischievous animal here is the small black sandfly which are exceeding numerous and are so troublesome that they exceed everything of the kind I have ever met with, wherever they light they cause a swelling and such an intolerable itching that it is not possible to refrain from scratching and at last ends in ulcers like the small pox'.

A Maori legend has it that the gods who created Fiordland were so pleased with their work that they sat back to relax and admire it; seeing this, the goddess of life and death, Hinenui te pou, created *te namu*, the sandfly, to goad them back to work. Apply insect repellent and if you are bitten try to refrain from scratching for 30 minutes – the itching will go away.

The other vital precaution to take is against sunburn. The clarity of the air in New Zealand allows more harmful ultraviolet rays to reach ground level than elsewhere, a situation that has intensified with the growing hole in the ozone layer over the Antarctic. Sunglasses and/or a hat should be worn outside, as well as plenty of sunblock, even on overcast days. Travellers arriving from winter in the Northern Hemisphere are particularly susceptible to sunburn unless adequately protected.

# WHAT TO SEE

'I thank God I was born in New Zealand. A young country is a real heritage, though it takes time to recognise it. But New Zealand is in my very bones. What wouldn't I give to have a look at it!'
**KATHERINE MANSFIELD,**
*letter to the Hon Dorothy Brett, 1922*

# AUCKLAND AND NORTHLAND

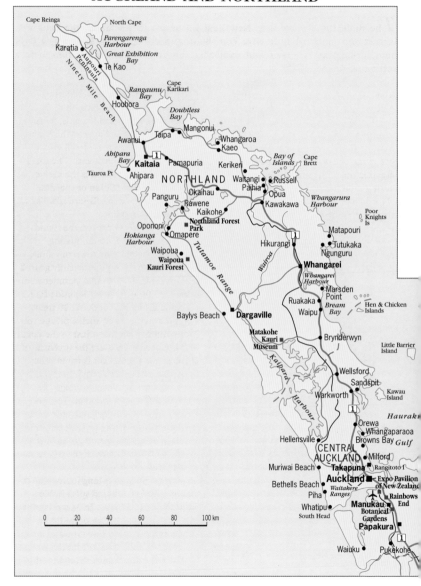

# Auckland and Northland

*T*he majority of visitors to New Zealand arrive in Auckland, the country's largest and most dynamic city. You should plan to spend at least a few days here, orientating yourself and exploring the city's many attractions before setting off further afield.

A logical starting point from Auckland is to head up towards Northland, the irregularly shaped, 240km-long peninsula that juts out at an odd angle from the North Island's top corner. Stretching out towards the Equator and bisecting the 35th parallel – hence putting it on the same latitude as Sydney – Northland revels in a mild climate which has earned it the nickname of the 'winterless North'.

Northland has a rich historical legacy that reflects its position as the birthplace of New Zealand. It was here that the first

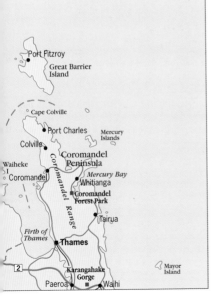

Polynesian explorers settled, later to be followed by the Europeans on their whaling ships. Ancient legends, tribal battles, and warfare between the Maori and European colonists are all woven into the fabric of Northland. The main resort area in Northland is the scenic Bay of Islands, where 800km of coastline shelter the 150 or so offshore islands that give the area its name.

There are no resorts on the islands themselves; most accommodation surrounds the bustling town of Paihia, a pleasant town which is efficiently geared up to cope with its annual summer influx of over 70,000 visitors. Alongside Paihia is Waitangi, the site of the 1840 treaty signing which formed such a pivotal role in the country's history. Just to the north of the Bay of Islands are the orchards of citrus and kiwifruit that surround the township of Kerikeri, which boasts two of the country's oldest buildings, one in stone and the other wooden. Their age, however, pales into insignificance when compared with nature's own work in the form of the magnificent *kauri* trees in the forests on the west side of the peninsula at Waipoua.

From Paihia it's a long journey up to one of the most isolated spots in New Zealand, Cape Reinga. In Maori legend this was just the starting point for an even longer journey, since it was from here that the spirits set off for the voyage back across the oceans to Hawaiki, the ancestral homeland.

# Auckland

$N$ew Zealand's largest city sprawls across the narrowest point of North Island and is almost completely surrounded by water: to the south and west, Manukau Harbour opens out into the Tasman Sea; to the north and east, Waitemata Harbour gives on to the Hauraki Gulf and, eventually, the Pacific.

The second most noticeable feature about Auckland is the volcanic cones that are dotted randomly around the city. There used to be over 50 volcanoes here, and when the district was most heavily populated by Maori tribes in the mid-18th century nearly every single one of these was home to a fortified settlement, or *pa*. Inter-tribal warfare brought this prosperous period to a close at the end of that century, and by the time Auckland was chosen as the new capital after the Treaty of Waitangi in 1840 the region was almost deserted. Eventually, 49 of these volcanic cones were used for landfill; the most prominent of those that remain (such as Mount Eden and One Tree Hill) provide spectacular viewpoints over the city. If you are visiting on a weekend, the panorama will undoubtedly reveal a flotilla of yachts cruising the harbour waters. Not for nothing is Auckland known as the 'City of Sails' – reputedly, there are more boats per person here than in any other city in the world.

Despite Auckland's urban sprawl, the proximity of vast stretches of coastline mean that deserted coves and surfing beaches are never more than a short drive (or sail) away; with the added bonus of an agreeable climate, many people feel that the Auckland lifestyle is one to be envied. In addition, the city can justifiably claim to be the most sophisticated and cosmopolitan in the country, with a wide range of cultural activities, world-class museums, hundreds of busy boutiques and shops, and scores of excellent restaurants and chic bars. The high-rise Sky Tower houses the the country's second casino, the Auckland Casino.

As the main international gateway for New Zealand, Auckland is the initial entry point for many visitors and a major export centre. In recent years the city has also become a focal point for Pacific Islanders, who have flocked here in search of work or to pursue higher education. As New Zealand builds on historic links and increasingly ties itself to other far-flung islands in the south seas, Auckland has cast itself in the role of 'hub of the Pacific'.

With around a quarter of the country's population (just over a million people) living within a 40km radius of the heart of the city you might think it would seem crowded, but Aucklanders have always preferred low-density housing where even the humblest home has its own garden – hence the sprawling suburbs. For the visitor, this has its drawbacks as, with the exception of the downtown area, it is not an easy city to get around without transport. Unless you have hired a car, the best options are either to buy a 'Busabout' pass (daily or weekly rates include unlimited rides) or use the Explorer Bus, which travels between six major attractions on an hourly basis.

Yachts, launches and ferries continually criss-cross Auckland's busy harbour

## AUCKLAND DOMAIN AND MUSEUM

The Domain is Auckland's biggest public park, comprising around 80 hectares of rolling lawns, gardens and a splendid subtropical conservatory known as the Wintergardens. At the centre is the Auckland Museum, originally built as a war memorial. Although it still houses war relics, the principal attraction now is the extensive display of Maori artefacts, including *Te Toki a Tapiri* ('Tapiri's Battle-axe'), an impressive 25m-long war canoe carved from a single tree trunk. Built in 1836, this was the last of the great Maori war canoes and could carry a hundred warriors. Other displays focus on natural history, Pacific culture and Asian art. The new 'Volcanoes and Giants' section will appeal to children, with its walk-in volcanoes, native New Zealand dinosaurs and animated models of extinct species such as the enormous moa and the New Zealand giant eagle.

Twice daily the museum hosts a guided tour of the Maori section, followed by live performances of Maori songs and dances. This combined tour and show is the best introduction you could find to Maori culture and is highly recommended.

*The Domain. Tel: 09 309 0443. Buses 635, 545–5, 655 from downtown (alight at Domain Drive).*
*Wintergardens open: daily 10am–4pm. Free.*
*Museum open: daily 10am–5pm. Free.*
*Maori tour/show: daily 10.30am and 12.45pm. Admission charge.*

## AUCKLAND ZOO

Linked to MOTAT 1 (see page 37) by a tramway, the zoo houses all the usual exotic creatures as well as native species such as the kiwi in a nocturnal house and indigenous birds in a forest aviary. A new African Pridelands development has opened. On weekends and holidays the keepers give regular talks at various enclosures.

*Motions Road, Western Springs. Tel: 09 360 3819. Open: daily 9.30am–5.30pm. Admission charge.*

## CITY ART GALLERY

The gallery is divided between two buildings. The Heritage Gallery, on the corner of Wellesley and Kitcher streets, houses more traditional works of art, including one of the country's best known artists, C F Goldie (1870–1947), who specialised in Maori portraits. The New Gallery, situated on the corner of Wellesley and Lorne streets, contains much more modern pieces with particular Maori influence and use of bright colours.

*Tel: 09 309 0831. Open: daily 10am–5pm. Guided tours. Free.*

## HOBSON WHARF NATIONAL MARITIME MUSEUM

Housed inside old warehouses surrounding a small marina, the new Hobson Wharf National Maritime Museum is an evocative celebration of the country's maritime heritage and the seagoing traditions of the South Pacific. It seems almost a shame to label this dynamic enterprise with the dusty old tag 'museum', so skilfully have traditional-style displays been woven together with workshops (including one which runs boat-building and restoration courses, as well as others housing sailmakers, riggers and wood-carvers), the marina itself (where canoes and veteran craft, including a brigantine and a scow, bob on the waves), sailing trips on board an old steam launch, and historic exhibits, such as the reconstruction of a steerage cabin on an early immigrant ship which sways and creaks convincingly as you explore its interior.

In addition, there is an outstanding collection of Pacific canoes, historic yachts and coastal vessels, and an intriguing passenger-shipping database where descendants of early immigrants can look up the names and dates of the ships their ancestors arrived on – the computer contains the details of nearly 100,000 arrivals. Another innovative feature is an 'oral history cabin' where shipwrecked sailors, whalers and lighthouse-keepers recount their experiences on tape.

*Corner Quay and Hobson streets. Tel: 09 373 0800. Open: daily 9am–5pm. Admission charge.*

## KELLY TARLTON'S ANTARCTIC ENCOUNTER AND UNDERWATER WORLD

Kelly Tarlton was a famous underwater explorer whose vision in later years was the building of his Underwater World. Sadly he died in 1985 just seven weeks after seeing his dream come true, but his legacy has turned out to be one of the country's most popular tourist attractions. The main feature of this underground aquarium is a circular acrylic tunnel with a moving walkway which carries you through large tanks teeming with fish, stingrays and several species of shark.

Underwater World has now been extended to include the Antarctic Encounter, which opened in 1993.

Inside, there is a brilliant replica of the hut used by Sir Robert Scott on his last, ill-fated expedition in 1910–12. The musty, gloomy interior (which even smells authentic) vividly re-creates the working lives and day-to-day pastimes of Scott's team in this harsh environment. After Scott's hut you board a snow cat for a taste of the Antarctic; highlights of this short journey include a simulated (and highly disorientating) white-out, a mock Orca whale which rises from the depths to devour a seal, and a real penguin colony.

*Orakei Wharf, 23 Tamaki Drive, Orakei, approximately 6km from the city centre. 'Kelly's coach' runs hourly from Britomart Terminal downtown, stopping at major hotels. Tel: 09 528 0603. Open: daily 9am–9pm (last admission 8pm) in summer (9am–6pm in winter). Admission charge.*

## MOUNT EDEN AND ONE TREE HILL

From the top of Mount Eden (Auckland's highest volcanic peak at 196m) there is a fabulous panorama of the city and its surrounding bays and harbours. This strategic point was once an important *pa* (fortified settlement), occupied soon after the landing by Polynesians in 1350, and ancient terracing is clearly visible around the summit.

One Tree Hill offers another (albeit less spectacular) viewpoint. One Tree Hill was an even bigger *pa* than Mount Eden, and terracing is also evident here.

*Mount Eden lies off Mount Eden Road. Bus 274, 275 from downtown. One Tree Hill lies off Manukau Road. Buses 300–319 from Queen Street and Victoria Street.*

With spectacular views over the city, Mount Eden is the highest volcanic peak in Auckland

# AUCKLAND ENVIRONS

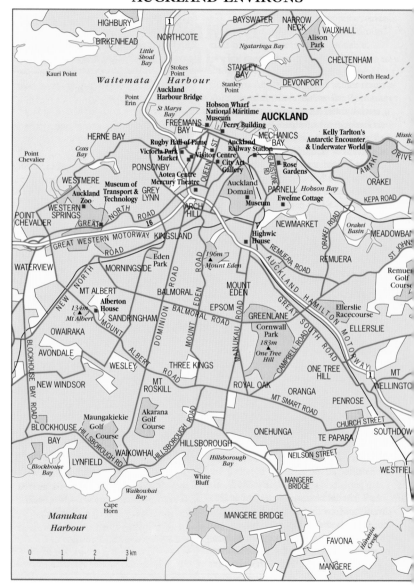

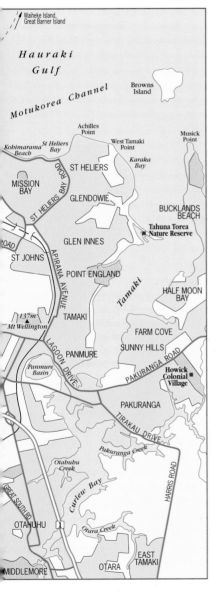

## MUSEUM OF TRANSPORT TECHNOLOGY AND SOCIAL HISTORY

The Museum of Transport Technology and Social History is spread over two different sites alongside the Auckland Zoo. The main site, MOTAT 1, contains exhibits ranging from vintage machinery and equipment to a historic beam engine. Of particular interest are the remains of the plane flown by Richard Pearce, the pioneering South Island aviator.

MOTAT 2 (1km away) has a fascinating collection of aircraft including the only Solent Mark IV flying boat left in the world.

*Great North Road, Western Springs. A tramway links MOTAT 1 with the zoo. Tel: 09 846 7020. Open: daily 10am–5pm. Admission charge.*

## PARNELL

Parnell is a trendy, gentrified suburb, one of Auckland's oldest, with a host of art galleries, up-market craft shops, bookshops and fashion boutiques, as well as over 40 cafés, restaurants, wine bars and pubs. At its heart is Parnell Village, a Victorian-style arcade of shopping enclaves and restored houses connected by boardwalks and little wooden bridges.

*30 minutes walk from downtown, or take bus 63, 64, or 65.*

## VICTORIA PARK MARKET

The present-day market is a rambling complex (around 1 hectare) with a wide range of shops and market stalls, as well as cafés, bars and outdoor eating areas. The market is particularly lively at weekends, when there are outdoor performances and live music.

*Victoria Street West and corner of Wellesley Street. Tel: 09 309 6911. Open: daily 9am–7pm.*

# HISTORIC HOUSES

New Zealand has a wealth of historic buildings ranging from the earliest surviving building, Kemp House in Kerikeri (see page 47), to old lighthouses and pioneer cottages. Auckland itself has several historic houses which can be visited conveniently in a single day.

### Highwic
This is one of New Zealand's finest houses in the timber Gothic style. Built by Alfred Buckland in 1862, it was designed in the early English style with steep slate roofs, vertical boarding, dormers and latticed casement windows. The house was expanded several times to accommodate Buckland's family (twice married, he fathered 20 children) and servants. The earlier part of the house is far less ornate and of simpler proportions than later additions, which reflect the High Victorian style with their excessive ornamentation, heavily embroidered furnishings and dark walls. Buckland died in 1903, and Highwic remained in the family until 1978.

### Alberton
Built in the same year as Highwic, Alberton was the home of Allan Kerr Taylor (1832–90), who made his fortune in farming and gold-mining. This grandiose mansion is unusual because of its Indian-style towers and imposing verandas. The interior is furnished in typical Victorian style.

Alberton is one of several historic homes surviving in Auckland

**Highwic,** 40 Gillies Avenue, Epsom (tel: 09 524 5729).
**Alberton,** 100 Mt Albert Road, Mt Albert (tel: 09 846 7367).
**Ewelme Cottage,** 14 Ayr Street, Parnell (tel: 09 379 0202).
All are open daily 10.30am–noon, 1–4.30 pm. Admission charge.
These houses are just three of the many properties in the country owned or administered by the Historic Places Trust (Pouhere Taonga in Maori) which also helps with the protection of Maori heritage sites. For more details, contact: New Zealand Historic Places Trust, PO Box 2629, Wellington.

### Ewelme Cottage

When Ewelme Cottage was built in 1864, the district of Parnell consisted mostly of open fields. Today the house stands surrounded by others in what is now a busy inner-city suburb, but it still embodies the feel of the pioneer lifestyle. Designed by a clergyman and his wife, Vicesimus and Blanche Lush, Ewelme was built using local *kauri* wood and is shingle-roofed. It was lived in by the Lush's descendants until 1968; nearly all the furniture and personal effects are original. Several rooms in Ewelme were used as sets for the Oscar-winning film *The Piano*.

# Auckland Environs

## BEACHES

There is a good selection of beaches along the coastline neighbouring Auckland and around the harbour. Travelling eastwards, Tamaki Drive runs along the shoreline past several fine beaches, such as Mission Bay, Kohimarama and St Heliers. On the North Shore there are many good beaches between Devonport and Long Bay, some of the more popular of these being Takapuna, Milford and Browns Bay, with Orewa further north. The West Coast is dominated by rolling surf off the Tasman Sea; some of the better-known surf beaches are Bethells, Whatipu, Piha and Muriwai. (Care must be taken at all times on this coast.)

## HAURAKI GULF

Nestling between the mainland and the Coromandel Peninsula to the east, the Hauraki Gulf is a popular yachting area. Most of it lies within the Hauraki Gulf Maritime Park, which encompasses 47 islands. Some of these islands can be reached on day-trips, while others are more remote and require additional time and energy to explore. Most of them are, however, serviced by regular ferries or light aircraft. A selection of the more popular islands includes the following:

### Great Barrier Island

The largest of the gulf islands, Great Barrier has a population of just over 1,000 people spread over 110sq km, and has plenty of unspoiled wilderness areas and beautiful beaches to explore. Excellent hiking trails and campsites make this a walker's paradise, while fishing, diving and kayaking are all possible around the extensive coastline. The wildest areas are in the northern section, which has many rare bird and plant species. The island has a handful of guest-houses and hostels in addition to the DOC campsites.

*The islands can be reached by fast ferry (tel: Fullers on 09367 9111). Great Barrier Airlines (tel: 09 275 9120) flies from Auckland several times daily. There is a DOC information centre at Port Fitzroy. Accommodation and activities can be booked in Auckland through the New Zealand Adventure Travel Services, PO Box 7011, Wellesley Street, Auckland.*

### Kawau Island

Tucked into the coastline above Auckland, Kawau's main attraction is the historic Mansion House; originally built by a mine manager, it was restored by Sir George Grey (one of the country's early governors) in the 1860s. The house and its exotic gardens are now open to the

The Mansion House on Kawau is surrounded by lovely gardens

Waiheke is just one of several islands in the Hauraki Gulf which can easily be visited from Auckland

public. Elsewhere on Kawau there are old copper mines, walking tracks and secluded beaches and picnic spots.

*Kawau Cat departs several times daily (journey time 45 minutes) from Sandspit, one hour's drive north of Auckland (tel: 09 425 8006). You can also join the Royal Mail Run (departs daily, 10.30am), which stops at all the bays and inlets to drop off mail. Mansion House, Kawau Island. Tel: 09 422 8882. Open: daily 10am–3.30pm. Admission charge.*

### Rangitoto Island

Rangitoto emerged from the sea around 600 years ago and is one of Auckland's youngest volcanoes. There are walking tracks across this intriguing volcanic landscape, as well as lava caves and fern groves to discover. The island has the largest remaining forest of *pohutukawa* trees in the country (see page 13), as well as over 200 species of native trees and flowering plants. There are terrific views from the 259m summit (allow an hour each way).

*The DOC visitor information kiosk has walking maps. Fullers Ferries run three times daily (summer) and twice daily in winter. Tel: 09 367 9102 for information.*

### Waiheke Island

Waiheke is one of the closest islands to Auckland. It has fine beaches and a variety of other attractions (from bush-walking tracks to vineyards, good restaurants and a thriving arts and crafts community) which make it popular with Aucklanders at weekends. Another reason for the island's popularity may be that it is reputed to be an average 5°C warmer than the mainland! Mountain biking, horse-riding and kayaking around the coast are all well provided for.

*Fullers Ferries run six times daily (journey time 35 minutes). Buses connect with ferry arrivals and departures.*

# Devonport

This is an easy walk through the historic settlement of Devonport, a short ferry ride across the harbour from central Auckland. The walk also takes in some fine views of the Hauraki Gulf and its islands. *Allow 2 to 3 hours.*

*Take a Fullers Ferry from the Downtown Ferry Terminal. On leaving the Devonport Wharf building, turn left along Queen's Parade. Turn right at the end, down Spring Street, to the Navy Museum.*

## 1 THE ROYAL NEW ZEALAND NAVY MUSEUM

This small museum has a rich collection of items relating to New Zealand's naval heritage, with a huge array of medals, models and memorabilia from various campaigns. There are also ships in bottles, a cat-o'-nine-tails, figure-heads and armaments.

*Retrace your steps and turn left up Victoria Road. Notice the elegant shop façades that have stood for over a hundred years.*

## 2 VICTORIA ROAD

This main thoroughfare is lined with bookshops, craft galleries, outdoor cafés and antique and souvenir shops. On the corner, commanding the seafront, is the Esplanade Hotel. Built in 1902, it was modelled on the popular English seaside hotels of the era.

*At the end of Victoria Road, keep going up the path which leads to the top of Mount Victoria, an extinct volcanic cone with the outline of ancient Maori fortifications clearly visible around the summit.*

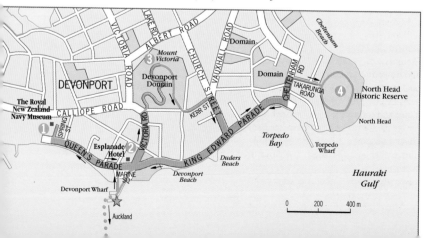

Mount Victoria rises up behind historic Devonport, a short ferry ride from the city centre

**The Royal New Zealand Navy Museum** – tel: 09 445 5186. Open: daily 10am–4.30pm. Free.
**North Head Historic Reserve**. Open: daily 6am–10pm. Free.
Fullers Ferries run at 20-minute intervals, 6am–11pm.
**Devonport Visitor Centre** Victoria Road. Open: daily 10am–4pm. Tel: 09 446 0677.

## 3 MOUNT VICTORIA

From Mount Victoria, which is 196m high, there are lovely views over Hauraki Gulf and its islands and back across the city and its harbour. There is an orientation table at the summit which enables you to identify the surrounding local landmarks; on a clear day the views extend as far as the Great Barrier Island and out to the Coromandel Peninsula. The outlines of terraces and pits can be distinguished on the hilltop, principally on the northern and eastern elevations.
*Follow the path back down the east side of the hill. Turn right at the end of Kerr Street to enter Church Street. At the seafront, turn left and follow the road round past the playing fields, turning right up Takarunga Road.*

## 4 NORTH HEAD HISTORIC RESERVE

North Head, like Mount Victoria, was a strategic *pa* (fortified settlement) due to its commanding views across any potential routes of attack. It became a military post in the late 19th century, when fears of a Russian invasion prompted the building of gun batteries; one of these housed an unusual 'disappearing gun' which recoiled underground after firing – it is just one of the defences that can still be seen today.

The whole hillside is riddled with ancient guns, searchlights, a network of old tunnels and other fortifications, most of which can be explored with the aid of a torch.
*Follow the road back along the seafront to return to Victoria Road and the ferry terminal.*

# Bay of Islands

*T*his is one of New Zealand's most historic regions, as well as being one of the North Island's most popular resort areas. Paihia, Waitangi and Russell are the three most important towns on the bay.

## PAIHIA AND WAITANGI

Paihia, the main hub for accommodation and excursions in the Bay of Islands, is a busy resort with numerous opportunities for boat trips, diving, swimming and yachting. Excursions to swim with dolphins are also popular, and Paihia is a major centre for deep-sea fishing.

Just over 2km from Paihia on the north side of the Waitangi river is the 506-hectare **Waitangi National Reserve**, at the centre of which is the historic Waitangi Treaty House. The Treaty House was the setting for the first signings of the Treaty of Waitangi (1840). The house itself, one of the country's oldest-surviving buildings, was completed in 1834 and was the home of James Busby, the first British Resident. The interior has been partially restored. Outside the house, overlooking the Bay of Islands, a huge flag-pole stands on the site where the treaty was signed. To one side is an unusual *whare runanga* (meeting-house), each of its 28 carved interior wall slabs representing a different group of tribes. A short walk away, on Hobson's Beach, is an impressive *waka* (war canoe); the 37m-long *Ngatokimatawhaorua* was built for the 1940 Centennial celebrations of the signing of the treaty. At the entrance to Waitangi National Reserve is a well-equipped visitor centre with half-hourly audio-visual presentations on the Treaty.

Half-way between Paihia and Waitangi is the **Museum of Shipwrecks**, housed on board the *Tui*, an old sailing ship built entirely of *kauri* wood. The museum houses artefacts dredged from the deep by Kelly Tarlton, a famous underwater explorer who died in 1985. His collection covers treasures brought up from more than 70 wrecks.
*Waitangi National Reserve, Paihia. Tel: 09 4027 308. Open: daily 9am–5pm. Admission charge.*
*Kelly Tarlton's Museum of Shipwrecks, Waitangi. Tel: 09 4027 018. Open: daily 10am–6pm. Admission charge.*

## RUSSELL

Russell's first outside settlers were ex-convicts and sailors who deserted from the whaling ships which stopped here in the early 19th century. By 1840 it was the largest European settlement in the country and a notorious frontier town, with no less than 40 'grog shops' and brothels. The missionaries called it the 'hell-hole of the Pacific'.

Today Russell is a tranquil township where life revolves around big-game fishing, messing about in boats and a handful of historic attractions. Prime amongst the latter is **Christ Church**, the oldest-surviving church in the country. The church still bears the marks of musket balls from an attack in 1845, and the churchyard contains many historic graves. Just across from the church is the **Russell Museum**, containing a wide range of memorabilia relating to maritime history and the early settlers, as well as a remarkable one-fifth scale reproduction of the *Endeavour*.

A key feature of the town is an unusual building known as **Pompallier House** (named after the first Catholic bishop of the South Pacific), an elegant two-storey house built by French missionaries for their printing presses. It is New Zealand's oldest-surviving industrial building and has been restored to its former role as a printing and book-binding works. There is a small shop where you can buy the beautiful volumes made here.

A short walk or drive up the hill above town brings you to Flagstaff Hill, with panoramic views of the Bay. Hone Heke Pokai, a Maori leader, chopped down the flagstaff – a symbol of the hated settlers – four times in the 1840s.

*Christ Church is on the corner of Church and Robertson streets.*

*Russell Museum, York Street. Open: daily 10am–5pm. Admission charge.*

*Pompallier House, The Strand. Tel: 09 403 7861. Open: daily 10am–5pm. Admission charge.*

*Ferries depart from Paihia wharf at regular intervals throughout the day (crossing time is 10 minutes).*

The sheltered harbour at Russell has been a haven for seafarers since whaling days

Ninety Mile Beach sweeps down the west coast of Northland from Cape Reinga

## CAPE REINGA

Cape Reinga is the most northerly point in New Zealand which can be reached by road (North Cape, which can be seen from here, is in fact 5km further north but there is no public access to it). From the promontory of Cape Reinga there are spectacular sea views, with the waves (sometimes reaching 10m in height) crashing over Colombus Reef just offshore where the Pacific Ocean and Tasman Sea meet. An integral part of all Cape Reinga tours is a trip back down the west side of the peninsula along Ninety Mile Beach. In fact, the beach is 90km long (the misunderstanding is attributed to a French explorer who merely marked '90' on his chart, subsequently interpreted as miles by the English). On the east side of the peninsula most tours also stop off at Houhora, where there is an extensive and well-displayed old collection of Victoriana, stuffed birds, shells and

Maori exhibits at the **Wagener Museum**, as well as an early pioneer house, the **Subritzky Homestead**, next door.

*Day-trips operate from Kaitaia and Paihia – the former is preferable, since the round-trip tour from Paihia is 500km.*

*Wagener Museum and Subritzky Homestead, Houhora. Tel: 09 409 8850. Open: daily 8.30am–4pm. Admission charge.*

*116km northwest of Kaitaia.*

## DOUBTLESS BAY

The first landing here was by the legendary Polynesian explorer, Kupe, in AD 950. In 1769, the *Endeavour* arrived here and the look-out boy shouted 'Land on three sides, Sir'. Cook replied 'Doubtless, a bay', and the name stuck. It has beautiful beaches (at Cable Bay, Cooper's Beach and Taipa) and is fast becoming a holiday-home centre. At the

eastern end of Doubtless Bay is the laid-back waterfront community of Mangonui, a former *kauri* export depot.
*Approximately 30km from Kaitaia.*

## HOKIANGA HARBOUR

The deep inlet of Hokianga Harbour on the western coastline of Northland presents one of those strange contrasts in landscape which are typical of New Zealand: on the southern spur of the harbour is deep forest, while the northern head consists of a single enormous sand dune rising up above the water. The harbour was in use in the early 19th century, but later developments passed it by and it is now a peaceful area where the main activities are fishing, boating and lazing on the beach. The two main settlements are Omapere and Opononi.
*80km northwest of Whangarei.*

## KAITAIA

The second largest town in Northland after Whangarei, Kaitaia has no particular attractions in its own right but is a useful base for visiting Cape Reinga to the north.
*160km north of Whangarei.*

The Kerikeri Basin, with two of New Zealand's oldest houses

## KERIKERI

Thanks to its fertile volcanic topsoil, the Kerikeri district is one of the richest agricultural areas in Northland and produces quantities of citrus fruit in the orchards that lie hidden away behind the tall hedges which line the roadsides. This small community has developed in recent years as a centre for pottery and handicrafts.

Kerikeri was the site of the country's second mission station, established here by the Reverend Samuel Marsden in 1819. The wooden **Kemp House**, built in 1822, stands above the picturesque Kerikeri inlet just behind the **Stone Store**, the oldest stone building in New Zealand (completed in 1835); the latter is still in use as a shop today, and has a small museum on its first floor. Just across the bridge over the inlet is **Rewa's Maori Village**, a full-scale replica of an old Maori fishing village.
*Kemp House – open: daily 10am–5pm (May to October, closed Thursday and Friday).*
*Stone Store Museum – open: daily 10am–5pm.*
*Rewa's Maori Village – open: daily 10am–4pm. Admission charge for all three.*

*23km north of Paihia.*

## MATAKOHE KAURI MUSEUM

*Kauri* logging was one of the most important industries in Northland at the turn of the century, reaching its peak between 1870 and 1910. This excellent museum traces the history of *kauri* logging, and displays include old milling equipment, a bushman's shanty and some gigantic *kauri* planks, the size of which (up to 8m long and over 2m wide) brings home exactly why this timber was so valuable. Adjoining rooms show the end result in the form of a re-created settler's house with *kauri* panelling and some fine pieces of *kauri* furniture. The museum also houses a huge collection of *kauri* gum in raw and worked form; this amber-coloured resin was once hugely popular as a craft medium.

An old log hauler outside the Kauri Museum in Matakohe

In the adjoining shop you can pick up small souvenirs made from swamp *kauri* (preserved tree trunks excavated from the swamps) which has been carbon-dated at around 44,000 years old.
*26km from the Brynderwyn junction on Highway 1 (signposted). Tel: 09 431 7417. Open: daily 9am–5pm. Admission charge.*

## WAIPOUA KAURI FOREST

In the Maori creation myth it is Tane Mahuta, Lord of the Forest, who brings light to the world by thrusting his feet upwards to separate Rangi (the Sky Father) from Papa (the Earth Mother). It is easy to imagine how this cosmology originated when you stand beside the awesome trunk of New Zealand's largest tree, named after Tane Mahuta, in the Waipoua Forest. Its height is impressive (over 50m) but it is really the girth (nearly 14m around) that gives such a

powerful impression of strength and longevity.

Tane Mahuta is just one of several massive *kauris* in the forest, all easily accessible by boardwalk from the main road (Highway 12) which runs through the forest. Near by are Te Matua Ngahere (Father of the Forest – the oldest *kauri* in the forest at about 2,000 years old), the Four Sisters (a grove of four graceful *kauris* growing close together) and the Yakas Kauri (30 minutes' walk from the road).

Waipoua and the neighbouring forests of Mataraua and Waima together make up the largest remaining tract of native forest in Northland, and are home to threatened species such as native forest parrots (*kakariki* and *kaka*) and the North Island brown kiwi. There are a number of marked walking trails through the forest, ranging from one to six hours in duration; information and route maps are available from the DOC visitor centre.

*2km off Highway 12, around 64km northwest of Dargaville. Open: daily. Free. The Waipoua Forest Visitor Centre, Private Bag, Dargaville. Tel: 09 439 0605.*

## WHANGAREI

Northland's only city, Whangarei, faces an extensive, sheltered harbour – one of the deepest in New Zealand – and the country's only oil refinery. Points of interest include **Claphams Clock Museum**, with over a thousand clocks and watches, and the **Quarry Craft Co-operative**, which has a good range of weavings, hand-dyed clothing and ceramics.

The **Whangarei Falls**, 6km outside town on the Ngunguru road, is a popular picnic spot. The 25m-high cascade tumbles into a bush-fringed pool and

The Whangarei Falls, a picturesque spot outside the city

there is a pretty walk down through native woodlands to the base, with another path continuing across a wooden bridge and up the other side again (a 20-minute circuit). You can swim in the pool above the falls.

*Claphams Clock Museum, Water Street, Cafler Park. Tel: 09 438 3993. Open: daily 9am–8pm summer, 10am–4pm winter. Admission charge.*

*Quarry Craft Co-operative, Selwyn Avenue. Open: daily 8am–5pm. Free.*

*174km north of Auckland.*

# EARLY EXPLORERS

In legends passed down from generation to generation, it was the great Polynesian voyager Kupe who discovered New Zealand, landing in the far north of the country around AD 950. He came from a homeland known to the Maori as 'Hawaiki', which is now thought to have been 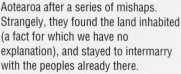 one of the Society Islands in East Polynesia. Kupe circled the islands, naming this new country Aotearoa, 'Land of the Long White Cloud'. He found no inhabitants, and eventually returned to Hawaiki with the sailing instructions which would enable others to follow.

Around 200 years later, Chief Toi and his grandson Whatonga ended up in

Aotearoa after a series of mishaps. Strangely, they found the land inhabited (a fact for which we have no explanation), and stayed to intermarry with the peoples already there.

In the 14th century a number of other canoes set off to look for Aotearoa in order to ease over-population in the Society Islands. At least 12 named canoes are known to have arrived, and even today many Maori tribes are known by the name of the canoe from which they claim descent.

Europeans had long speculated on the existence of an undiscovered land mass in the southern hemisphere, and in 1642 the Dutch East India Company ordered Abel Janszoon Tasman to look for this missing continent. On 13 December he became the first European to set eyes on the country when he spied land near Hokitika. He sailed north and anchored in Golden Bay, but a brief skirmish with the Maori convinced him not to land and he put back to sea.

In 1768 Captain James Cook sailed in the *Endeavour* to Tahiti, where he opened the 'secret instructions' which ordered him to proceed to New Zealand. The *Endeavour* arrived in Gisborne on 9 October, 1769, but a hostile encounter with the Maori forced him to sail away again.

Apart from the initial misunderstanding at Gisborne, Cook found the Maori friendly and helpful, and his accounts of this rich, fertile land and its hospitable people created a huge amount of interest in Europe.

Maori seafarers discovered New Zealand some 800 years before Captain Cook

# Central North Island

*T*he central North Island encompasses a wide variety of landscapes and contrasting destinations. Lying across the Hauraki Gulf from Auckland, the Coromandel Peninsula is more popular with city-dwellers than tourists, but this is fast changing as its superb beaches, laid-back lifestyle and rugged scenery become better known.

Coromandel's east coast merges into the Bay of Plenty. Here, too, the beaches are a major attraction (particularly for 'surfies') and the seas offshore are renowned for big-game fishing.

Beyond the Bay of Plenty's coastal resorts are the wild and sparsely populated coastlines of the East Cape, leading round into Poverty Bay and Gisborne, the most easterly city in the country. Hawke's Bay, south of Gisborne is well known for its wines and long hours of sunshine – the pleasant seaside city of Napier in Hawke's Bay is famous for its art deco architecture, as is neighbouring Hastings.

Volcanic activity is never far away in the North Island, and Lake Taupo, created by massive eruptions in the past, is a prime example. New Zealand's main geothermal area lies slightly to the north of Taupo, focused on the city and lake of Rotorua.

To the south of Lake Taupo, the volcanic belt reaches its southernmost point beneath the peaks of the Tongariro National Park. Finally, no tour of central North Island would be complete without a visit to the Waitomo Caves.

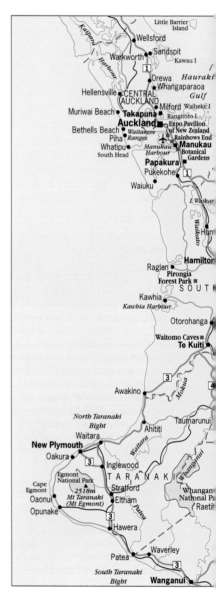

# CENTRAL NORTH ISLAND

# Bay of Plenty

## MOUNT MAUNGANUI

The resort of Mount Maunganui lies on the east side of Tauranga Harbour, straddling a narrow peninsula. The Mount itself overlooks the township and its beaches. There are walking trails around the 232m-high Mount (once an important *pa*, or fortified settlement) and hot salt-water pools at the base of the hill. The long, sandy, oceanside beach is popular for swimming, surfing and body-surfing.

*Accessible by bus or car across the harbour bridge from Tauranga.*

## TAURANGA

The city of Tauranga lies at the western end of the Bay of Plenty, and is a busy commercial centre whose prosperity is founded on the citrus trees and kiwifruit that grow on the fertile areas inland, and on Tauranga Harbour, the largest port in the country for exports. Tauranga was the scene of some bloody battles during the Land Wars (most notably the Battle of Gate Pa). During the fighting, the local missionary, Archdeacon Brown, tended the wounded of both sides; the house he completed in 1847, **Elms Mission House**, can be visited. The garden (planted in the 1830s) is one of the oldest in the country and contains a picturesque library and a reconstruction of the original tiny chapel.

The city's other main historical attraction is the **Tauranga Historic Village/Museum**, with its many relocated and restored old buildings. Among the exhibits are a re-creation of the 'Main Street' of yesteryear, displays of ancient radios, a Maori village and a steam train.

Back in the city centre, don't miss the Te Awanui war canoe resting in its shelter at the top end of the Strand. Built entirely from *kauri* wood, this replica is often paddled out into the harbour during ceremonial occasions.

*Elms Mission House, Mission Street. Tel: 07 578 9763. Gardens open: Monday to Saturday 9am–6pm. Guided tours: 2pm. Free.*

*Tauranga Historic Village/Museum, 155 17th Avenue West. Tel: 07 578 1302. Open: daily 9am–6pm. Admission charge.*

*88km north of Rotorua.*

## TE PUKE

Dubbed the 'kiwifruit capital of the world', Te Puke is where the first kiwifruit vines were planted in 1937. You can learn all about this fuzzy fruit at **Kiwifruit Country**, a horticultural theme park with rides through the orchards, visits to the

A giant kiwifruit near Te Puke

Young surfers on the popular ocean beach at Mount Maunganui, across the harbour from Tauranga

packing sheds, tastings of kiwifruit wines and other activities.

*Kiwifruit Country, Box 541, Te Puke. On the main Rotorua–Tauranga road (Highway 33), 6km south of Te Puke. Tel: 07 573 6340. Open: daily 9am–6pm. Admission charge.*

*31km southeast of Tauranga.*

## WHAKATANE

At the opposite end of the Bay of Plenty to Tauranga is Whakatane, another popular holiday base with a long, sweeping beach over the headland at Ohope. In the town itself is the diminutive **Whakatane District Museum and Gallery**, displaying Maori tools, cloaks, flaxwork, weapons and ornaments that belonged to the descendants of the Polynesians who landed here in the *Mataatua* canoe around AD 1350. Whakatane is noted for its deep-sea fishing and is the main access point for White Island (see below), just offshore.

*Whakatane District Museum and Gallery, Boon Street. Tel: 07 307 9805. Open: weekdays 10am–4.30pm, Saturday 11am–1.30pm, Sunday and public holidays 2–4.30pm. Admission charge.*

*100km southeast of Tauranga.*

## WHITE ISLAND

Visible on a clear day from Whakatane, White Island is an active volcano which smoulders away 50km off shore. Sulphur deposits were mined here from the 1870s until 1934, and the abandoned workings are now one of the curiosities to be seen alongside the active craters, sulphur vents, boiling pools and huge gannet colonies.

*Scenic flights to White Island are operated by Vulcan Helicopters, PO Box 10, Waimana (tel: toll-free 0800 804 354). All-day cruises are operated by the Pee Jay, (tel: 07308 0303 – toll-free 0800 733 529).*

# Coromandel Peninsula

**COLVILLE**

The last settlement in the northern Coromandel on the scenic cape route (see page 75).

**COROMANDEL**

This delightful township at the base of the Coromandel Range has become a magnet for craftspeople and those seeking 'alternative' lifestyles, as well as the focus of anti-mining campaigns in the peninsula. The town and peninsula were named after HMS *Coromandel*, which called in for *kauri* spars in 1820. In 1852 New Zealand's first gold finds were made here and 300 prospective miners flooded in from Auckland. However, the boom

proved premature, and it wasn't until the late 1860s that viable gold reefs were discovered. Those first gold strikes were made at Driving Creek, now the site of the **Driving Creek Railway and Potteries**. The narrow-gauge railway, built by potter Barry Brickell to bring clay down from the hills to his kilns, now serves a dual purpose as a tourist attraction with the 'station' lying in the middle of his potteries yard.

Just near Driving Creek, the methods used to separate gold from quartz are demonstrated at the restored **Coromandel Stamper Battery**, one of the first such works to be built in New Zealand. Early mining tools, rock samples and various colonial artefacts are on display in the **Coromandel Mining and Historical Museum**, housed in the original School of Mines building.

Most of the craft workshops around Coromandel welcome visitors; their locations are listed in the 'Coromandel Craft Trail' leaflet, available from the information centre.

There is an impressive grove of trees on Highway 309, some 15km from Coromandel.

*Driving Creek Railway and Potteries, 3km north of town. Tel: 07 866 8703. Trains run at 10am and 2pm all year, and also at noon and 4pm in summer. Admission charge.*
*Coromandel Stamper Battery, 2km north of town. Tel: 07 866 7186. Open: 10am–5pm in summer (weekends only in winter). Admission charge.*
*Coromandel Mining and Historical Museum, Rings Road. Open: 10am–3pm in*

An old wooden building in Thames, the main town in the Coromandel

summer (weekends
only in winter).
Admission charge.
Information centre,
355 Kapanga Road.
Tel: 07 866 8598.
Open: weekdays
9am–5pm, Saturday
10am–noon (later in
summer).

55km north of
Thames.

## THAMES

Thames was built
on the exploitation
of gold and *kauri* in
the late 19th
century, and used to
be one of the largest

Cattle graze the lowland slopes of the Coromandel Ranges

towns in New Zealand with a population
of 18,000 and over 70 working gold
mines in the vicinity. It is now the
principal gateway and shopping centre for
the Coromandel Peninsula. The gold
bonanza days are recalled in the
**Historical Museum**, whilst the nearby
**Mineralogical Museum** has one of the
largest collections of minerals and fossils
in the country. The Hauraki Prospectors
Association runs tours through the Gold
Mine and Stamper Battery just outside
Thames; alternatively, details of a three-
hour bush walk along Rocky's Goldmine
Trail are available from the town's
information centre.
*Historical Museum, corner of Pollen and*
*Cochrane streets. Open: daily 1–4pm.*
*Admission charge.*
*Mineralogical Museum, corner of Brown*
*and Cochrane streets. Open: Tuesday to*
*Sunday 11am–4pm. Admission charge.*
*Gold Mine and Stamper Battery, PO Box*
*133, on the northern outskirts of town.*

*Thames Visitor Centre – tel: 07 868 7284*
*for more details. Admission charge.*

*119km southeast of Auckland.*

## WHITIANGA

Whitianga is a busy summer resort town
in Mercury Bay on the peninsula's east
coast. The resort is renowned for its
fishing (particularly game fishing, which
peaks during February and March),
water sports and beaches. There are
numerous good swimming beaches near
by, plus the novelty of Hot Water Beach
at the mouth of the Tauwaiwe river to the
south, where you can dig your own spa
pool in the sand. From Whitianga's
wharf, ferries ply back and forth to Ferry
Landing, site of the original settlement on
the other side of the Narrows, from
where you can walk or cycle to a number
of lovely beaches and look-out points
over Mercury Bay.
*95km north of Thames.*

## EAST CAPE

The East Cape coastline encompasses some of the most dramatic and unspoiled scenery in the North Island. For many years the rugged Raukumara Range – which runs down the centre of the cape – made transport difficult, and the Maori who lived here were left in peace. Even though a 344km coastal road from Opotiki to Gisborne has since been built, the region remains quiet and laid back, with small Maori communities dotted along the coast between a succession of beautiful coves and beaches.

## GISBORNE

This is the first city in New Zealand to see the sun rise every day; its other claim to fame is as the site of Captain Cook's first landfall on 9 October, 1769. Cook's men unfortunately mistook the Maoris' *haka* (challenge) as an attack, and promptly shot them; further misunderstandings led to several more Maori deaths before the *Endeavour* sailed away. Cook named the spot Poverty Bay 'because it afforded us not one thing we wanted'.

Poverty Bay was, in fact, a complete misnomer, since the fertile plains around Gisborne are dotted with market gardens, maize fields and vineyards (see page 168). Cook's landing site is marked by

A statue of Captain Cook at Gisborne

an obelisk on the north side of the Turanganui river, and his statue gazes landwards from the top of Titirangi Hill above the port.

Near the town centre on the riverbank is the **Museum and Arts Centre**, which includes a number of interesting *tuhanga* (treasures) in its changing displays of Maori culture and colonial history. Behind the main museum is the **Maritime Museum**, housed inside the bridgehouse of *The Star of Canada*, which was wrecked on the beach here in 1912.

*Museum and Arts Centre and Maritime Musuem, 18–20 Stout Street. Tel: 06 867 3832. Open: weekdays 10am–4pm, weekends and public holidays. 1.30–4pm. Admission charge.*

*216km northeast of Napier.*

## HAMILTON

This prosperous city, a centre for the rich farmlands of the Waikato district, sits on New Zealand's longest river, the Waikato. Behind Hamilton's gleaming new buildings lie several scenic riverside parks, and you can also cruise along the Waikato on the old paddle-steamer, MV *Waipa Delta*.

The **Waikato Museum of Art and History** houses an extensive collection of artefacts from the local Tainui people, including the war canoe *Te Winika*, built in 1836, and contemporary Tainui carvings, a large collection of historic photographs and

The MV *Waipa Delta* cruises the Waikato River from the city of Hamilton

excellent displays of modern art.
*The MV Waipa Delta cruises for lunches, teas and dinner (tel: 07 854 9415 for information and bookings).*
*Waikato Museum, corner of Grantham and Victoria streets. Tel: 07 838 6533. Open: daily 10am–4.30pm. Admission charge.*

*129km south of Auckland.*

## HASTINGS

Hastings, sister township to Napier (see page 60) in Hawke's Bay, has none of the latter's charms and far fewer art deco buildings to see in its tawdry town centre. The main attraction lies just outside town at the family-oriented **Fantasyland**, a 23-hectare park with castles, pirate ships, train rides and many other amusements.

Beyond Hastings at the southernmost extremity of Hawke's Bay is **Cape Kidnappers**, one of the few mainland nesting sites for the striking Australian gannet, which congregates here in large numbers between July and April. You can visit the gannet colonies from mid-October to April (closed from July to mid-October to prevent disturbance).
*Fantasyland, Grove Road. Tel: 06 876 9856. Open: weekdays 9am–4.30pm, weekends 9am–5am. Admission charge; children free. Charge for cinema and some rides.*
*Information on the gannet colony is available from the DOC Centre, 59 Marine Parade, Napier. Tel: 06 835 0415. Open: daily, 9am–4.15pm. Gannet-viewing tours are operated by Gannet Beach Adventures, Charlton Road, Te Awanga. Tel: 06 875 0898. Open: daily. Admission charge.*

*236km south of Gisborne.*

Napier was almost completely rebuilt in classical art deco style after a massive earthquake

## NAPIER

Lying at the southern end of Hawke's Bay, Napier might have remained a rather humdrum seaside resort were it not for the events of 3 February, 1931, when most of the township was levelled by a massive earthquake, measuring 7.9 on the Richter scale. A total of 256 people died. The surviving residents set about rebuilding with unprecedented vigour, and within two years a completely new town had risen from the rubble. The architects involved adopted art deco or Spanish Mission styles (in vogue in America at the time), and the result is a town with a wealth of classic, 1930s-style features which have been carefully preserved to this day. The best way to explore Napier's art deco heritage is on a guided walking tour (see opposite), or, alternatively, by taking a stroll through the streets using the detailed leaflet 'Take an Art Deco Walk'.

The story of the earthquake is related in an audio-visual exhibit at **Hawke's Bay Museum**, which also has a good selection of decorative arts from the 1930s and a well-designed exhibition of carvings from the Ngati Kahungunu peoples of the east coast.

Napier's seafront esplanade, Marine Parade, is a broad avenue lined with Norfolk pines; it has several attractions including **Kiwi House**, **Marineland**, the **Napier Aquarium**, and various gardens. The earthquake story is also retold (complete with 14 seconds of simulated earthquake) at the **Stables Complex**, which includes a waxworks museum.

*All the attractions listed are within a few*

*minutes' walk of each other along Marine*
*Parade (admission charge for each).*
*Hawke's Bay Museum – tel: 06 835 7781.*
*Open: daily 10am–4.30pm.*
*Kiwi House – tel: 06 834 1336. Open: daily*
*11am–3pm.*
*Marineland – tel: 06 834 4027. Open: daily*
*10am–4.30pm.*
*Napier Aquarium – tel: 06 834 1404. Open:*
*daily 9am–5pm.*
*Stables Complex – tel: 06 835 1937. Open:*
*daily 9am–5pm.*
*Guided walking tours: Saturdays, Sundays*
*and Wednesdays at 2pm from the Art Deco*
*Shop, 163 Tennyson Street (tel: 06 835*
*0022). 'Take an Art Deco Walk', with a*
*self-guide walk map, costs NZ$1.50 from the*
*Art Deco Shop, Hawke's Bay Museum or the*
*visitor centre.*

*216km southwest of Gisborne.*

## OTOROHANGA

This small town on the way to the
Waitomo Caves (see page 72) is worth
a stop for the **Kiwi
House** and **Native
Bird Park** (just off the
main road). Here there
is a nocturnal house
with brown kiwis, a
water-bird section and a
huge, walk-in aviary
with native forest birds
such as the kea, tui and
kaka.
*Kiwi House and Native*
*Bird Park, Alex Tefler*
*Drive. Tel: 07 873 7391.*
*Open: daily 9.30am–5pm*
*(4pm in winter).*
*Admission charge.*

*60km south of Hamilton*
*on Highway 3.*

## UREWERA NATIONAL PARK

This is the third-largest national park in
New Zealand, covering just over 200,000
hectares of untamed forests in the
Urewera Range and is the largest
untouched stretch of native forest in the
North Island, with more than 650 types of
native plant. A haven for birdlife, Urewera
shelters many notable species, including
kaka and kakariki, plus the New Zealand
robin, New Zealand falcon and rifleman.
Deer, possums and pigs are actively
hunted.

At the centre of the park is the
magnificent Lake Waikaremoana ('Sea of
Shining Water'), almost entirely
surrounded by bush, except on the south
side, which is dominated by the dramatic
Panekiri Bluff. Following the shoreline for
most of its 51km length, the Lake
Waikaremoana Track takes three to four
days to walk and is one of the most
popular in the North Island. Information
on short walks is available from the visitor
centre at Aniwaniwa.

*Waikaremoana and*
*Aniwaniwa are*
*accessible via SH38,*
*which runs from Wairoa*
*on Hawke's Bay*
*through to Murupara*
*(to join the SH5 near*
*Rotorua). InterCity*
*buses operate from*
*Rotorua to Wairoa on*
*Monday, Wednesday*
*and Friday.*
*Aniwaniwa Visitor*
*Centre, Private Bag*
*2213, Wairoa. Tel: 06*
*837 3803. Open: daily*
*8am–5pm.*

An art deco window
in Napier

# Rotorua

*R*otorua is at the centre of what is known as the Taupo Volcanic Belt, which runs all the way from Tongariro National Park in the south to White Island in the Bay of Plenty. This volcanic action is, however, most evident in Rotorua: even if you don't notice the steam escaping from back gardens, road drains or rocky patches, your nose will certainly warn you of the ever-present smell of hydrogen sulphide (like rotten eggs) which wafts over the city.

The area was first inhabited by the Arawa tribe in the 14th century after they had made their way inland from the point at which their canoe beached in the Bay of Plenty. Once settled, they used the boiling volcanic pools for cooking and heated their houses (*whare*) naturally by building them on warm soil. During the 19th century the Arawa were almost

Thermal pools are one way of relaxing in Rotorua

constantly at war with neighbouring tribes, but once these local feuds ceased during the 1870s tourists started coming here for cures in the thermal waters and Rotorua took off as a spa town.

The first building in the new resort was the Tudor-style **Bath House**, built in 1907, which still stands today at the centre of Government Gardens on the shores of the lake. It is now home to the Rotorua Art and History Museum, which features several interesting permanent exhibitions. The two most important of these are 'In the Shadow of the Volcano', which tells the story of Tarawera Mountain and the fatal eruption on 10 June 1886 (see Te Wairoa Buried Village, page 66), and 'Nga Taonga o Te Arawa' (The Treasures of the Arawa People), which includes many superb and unusual carvings and important artefacts.

Near by is the **Polynesian Spa**, comprising 30 different pools (including eight hot mineral springs) in the garden. These are said to be especially helpful for rheumatism and arthritis as they have a high acidic content. There are also several private spa pools and a large mineral pool (with high alkalinity) for families and children. Also close by are the **Orchid Gardens**, featuring a cavernous indoor display of orchids, ferns

The Bath House in Rotorua's Government Gardens now houses the city's Art and History Museum

and other tropical and subtropical species, Microworld (with remote-control cameras trained on geckos, frogs and insects) and a rather mindless water organ with 700 water jets playing to synchronised music and coloured lights.

Further along, on the lakeside, is a quay from where you can explore Lake Rotorua and Mokoia Island on a paddle-steamer, cruise boat, jet hydrofoil, or by float plane or helicopter. A short walk past the quay is Ohinemutu, a Maori village which was once the main settlement on the lake before the spa town developed. Main attractions are a Tudor-style Anglican church, St Faith's (whose graveyard contains a number of important tombs), and a richly carved meeting-house, Tamatekapua, opposite the church named after the captain of the Arawa canoe.

For other attractions in the area (see pages 64–7), you will need your own transport, or you can hop on and off the Sightseeing Shuttle, which includes all the city centre sights and several of those on the outskirts. Passengers can leave at any stop and catch any following bus.

*Museum and Art Gallery, Government Gardens. Tel: 07 348 4199. Open: daily 9.30am–5pm. Admission charge.*

*Polynesian Spa, Hinemoa Street. Tel: 07 348 1328. Open: daily 6.30am–11pm. Admission charge.*

*Orchid Gardens, Hinemaru Street. Tel: 07 347 6699. Open: daily 8.30am–5.30pm. Admission charge.*

*Sightseeing Shuttle (8.15am–5.15pm – tel: 02 595 7399). Children half-price.*

*221km southeast of Auckland.*

# Rotorua Environs

## AGRODOME AND RAINBOW FARM

Both of these locations offer a similar type of experience – essentially a one-hour show about sheep. If you thought sheep were too boring to merit such coverage, then think again! The shows are highly

Sheep are the stars in entertaining farm shows around Rotorua

entertaining, and as well as explaining the differences between up to 19 different varieties of sheep on display, there is a sheep-shearing demonstration, a mock sheep auction, lamb-feeding and plenty of audience participation. Both offer farm tours and horse treks; the Agrodome also has a model railway display.

*Agrodome, Riverdale Park, Western Road, Ngongotaha, 7km northwest of Rotorua city centre on Highway 5. Tel: 07 357 4350. Shows: daily 9.30am, 11am and 2.30pm. Admission charge.*

*Rainbow Farm, Ngongotaha, 5km north from Rotorua city centre on Highway 5. Tel: 07 347 8104. Shows: daily 10.30am, 11.45am, 1pm and 2.30pm. Admission charge.*

## HELL'S GATE

In 1934 the English playwright George Bernard Shaw visited Hell's Gate and is reputed to have said: 'Hell's Gate, I think, is the most damnable place I have ever visited, and I'd willingly have paid ten pounds not to have seen it.' Quite why this sensitive soul was so upset by a few boiling sulphur cauldrons is perhaps a matter for theologians, but children (and probably adults too) will love the walk through Hell's Gate, where they can wonder at the bubbling pools, sulphurous jets of steam, boiling whirlpools, mud volcanoes and 'plopping liquids' in this 10-hectare reserve. Notices warn of the dire consequences of stepping off the path – temperatures in some pools reach 115°C.

*Hell's Gate, Tikitere, Rotorua, 16km from the city centre on Highway 30. Tel: 07 345 3151. Open: daily 9am–5pm. Admission charge.*

## PARADISE VALLEY SPRINGS

Similar in concept to the Rainbow and Fairy Springs (see opposite) but less crowded, Paradise Valley Springs also has trout pools, native flora and fauna (including a wetlands area for New Zealand water-birds) and other animals on display.

_Paradise Valley Springs, Paradise Valley Road, 11km from the city centre, signposted off Highway 5. Tel: 07 348 9667. Open: daily 8am–5pm. Admission charge._

## RAINBOW AND FAIRY SPRINGS

Fairy Springs first opened to the public in 1898 and is one of the most powerful natural springs in the region, gushing forth at the rate of around 23 million litres of water per day. The smaller Rainbow Springs flows at the rate of around 4.5 million litres per day; both are now part of a massive tourist complex which includes trout pools, native flora and fauna, and a nocturnal kiwi house. Hundreds of rainbow trout swim upstream from Lake Rotorua to spawn in the Rainbow Spring pools, and these are supplemented by juveniles reared in hatchery pools here. The pools are shaded by the deep green fronds of ferns and tree ferns.

The complex includes displays of animals introduced to New Zealand (such as deer, Himalayan thar and the massive 'Captain Cooker', a pig species brought here by Cook over 200 years ago) and native birds (like the kea and the kaka parrots), New Zealand woodpigeons (kereru), the mellifluous tui and the Paradise duck. It also serves as a conservation and breeding centre for protected species such as kiwis and the endangered kokako. A souvenir shop, a restaurant and the adjoining Rainbow Farm (see opposite) complete the facilities.

_Rainbow Springs, Fairy Springs Road, Auckland Highway, 5km north from the city centre on Highway 5. Tel: 07 347 9301. Open: daily 8am–5pm. Admission charge._

Rainbow trout swim upstream to spawn in the clear waters of the Rainbow Springs

## TE WAIROA BURIED VILLAGE

In the mid-19th century, Rotorua was famous not only as a spa centre but also for its fabulous Pink and White Terraces, a celebrated attraction of fan-like silica formations on the shores of Lake Rotomahana, usually visited by canoe from the Maori village of Te Wairoa.

However, on the morning of 10 June, 1886, Mount Tarawera (previously thought to be dormant) exploded, burying the villages of Te Wairoa, Moura and Te Ariki in nearly 3m of ash, lava and mud. Some 153 people died, and the famous Pink and White Terraces were obliterated for ever.

Parts of Te Wairoa have since been excavated, including the hut of the local *tohunga* (priest), who predicted the disaster and who was buried alive here for four days. Other remnants include the old Rotomahana Hotel and an unusual stone storehouse with carvings on the lintels – very rare in New Zealand, since Maori seldom carved in stone. There is a new museum complex which contains fascinating displays, as well as a waterfall trail.

*15km east of the city centre, on the Tarawera road. Tel: 07 362 8287. Open: daily from 9am. Admission charge.*

## WAIMANGU VOLCANIC VALLEY

This is another impressive volcanic area, with all the different attractions visible on a pleasant, downhill walk to Lake Rotomahana (around an hour one way; a free bus carries you back up again). The main sights include Frying Pan Lake (the world's largest hot spring), the former site of Waimangu Geyser, and Inferno Crater (which contains a steaming, pale-blue lake).

*23km south of Rotorua on Highway 5, signposted off the main road. Tel: 07 366 6137. Open: daily 8.30am–5pm. Admission charge.*

## WAIOTAPU THERMAL WONDERLAND

Billed as the country's 'most colourful thermal area', Waiotapu ('Sacred Waters') is worth the journey out from Rotorua city if only to see how natural chemicals have rendered an incredible range of tints and hues in thermal zones such as the Champagne Pool and the Artist's Palette. Near by is the Lady Knox Geyser which is 'soaped' every day at 10.15am (the soap acts to disperse the upper layers of water, thus allowing the

The brilliant colours of the Champagne Pool at the Waiotapu Thermal Wonderland

Volcanic activity is the main attraction at the unpronounceable Whakarewarewa Thermal Reserve

super-heated steam to burst through from the reservoir below); even so, the performance of the geyser is unpredictable. If there is enough water in the reservoir, Lady Knox can reach heights of around 20m and play for an hour; if not, it might only fizzle briefly to a height of around 5m.

*30km south of Rotorua on Highway 5, signposted off the main road. Tel: 07 366 6333. Open: daily 8.30am–4.30pm. Admission charge.*

## WHAKAREWAREWA THERMAL VILLAGE

'Whaka' (as most people call it) is the closest of the major thermal reserves to Rotorua city centre, and is best known for its twin geysers which spout forth at regular intervals. The first (and smallest) of these is the Prince of Wales Feathers, which reaches heights of around 12m and always precedes the eruption of its

neighbour, Pohutu (Maori for 'splashing'), which can reach heights of up to 20 to 30m, playing sometimes for 20 minutes or more. Near by are various silica formations, boiling pools and a Maori village.

Incorporated within the reserve is the New Zealand Maori Arts and Crafts Institute, set up in the 1960s to rejuvenate the dying art of Maori wood-carving. One of the first tasks of the artisans was to produce the carvings in the Te Aronui a Rua meeting-house, where afternoon concerts are now held daily at 12.15pm. Maori carvers can be seen at work inside the institute, where there is a gallery with finished pieces.

*Hemo Road, Rotorua, 3km from the city centre. Whakarewarewa Thermal Village Tel: 07 349 3463. Open: daily 8.30am–5pm. Admission charge. Maori Arts and Crafts Institute. Tel: 07 348 9047. Open: daily 8am–5pm. Admission charge.*

# MAORI SOCIETY

Traditional Maori society was organised into *whanau* (extended family groups), then *hapu* (sub-tribes, made up of several *whanau*), and finally the *iwi* (tribes). The *whanau* were ruled over by *kaumatua* and *kuia*, the male and female elders, who were in turn subject to the *ariki* (chiefs) of the *hapu* and the word of the *tohunga*, the priests who were entrusted with the secrets of tribal lore.

Every facet of Maori life was regulated by the dual concepts of *tapu* ('sacred', from which we derive 'taboo') and *mana* (which relates to prestige, pride and dignity). Any slight to one's *mana* had to be met with *utu* (retribution), a social code that gave rise to incessant inter-tribal conflict – although

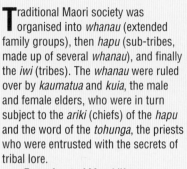

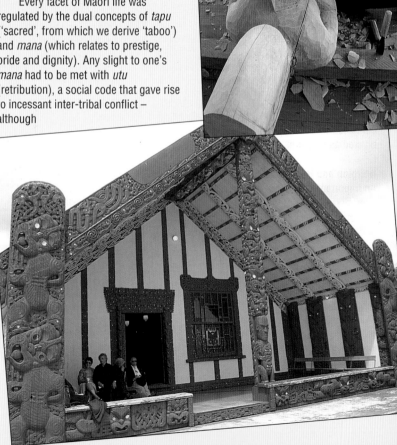

Many aspects of traditional Maori culture, such as carving, survive today. Right: fearsome facial expressions during the *peruperu* (war dance)

this was only seasonal, and war didn't take place when the *kumara* (sweet potato) crops needed attention.

The constant fighting meant that principal villages were often located on hilltops and were fortified; many hills still bear the distinctive terracing which marks the ramparts and ditches surrounding *pa* (hill forts).

At the centre of all villages was the *marae*, an open courtyard which served as a focal point for community life. Facing the *marae* was the *whare runanga* (meeting-house), which was often elaborately carved to represent the spirit of famous ancestors and contained tribal artefacts revered as treasures.

### Religion and legends

An important part of Maori cultural heritage is their vast store of imaginative and colourful legends, which were passed down from generation to generation. Maori mythology reveals a depth of thought and religious feeling which is closely tied in with their animist beliefs and reverence for nature. Traditionally, Maori worshipped many gods and goddesses, although unlike other Pacific peoples, they also believed in a 'supreme being', Io. This concept made it much easier for them to adapt to Christianity in the 19th century, which many did.

### Language

When spoken fluently, the Maori language is highly allegorical and riven with ancestral and spiritual references. Inevitably, usage has fallen away in recent years, but a campaign has begun for greater use of Maori in everyday life and 1995 was designated Maori Language Year.

# Taupo and Lake Taupo

*T*he resort town of Taupo enjoys a spectacular setting on the shores of Lake Taupo, looking towards Tongariro National Park, with the distant peaks of the park visible across the broad expanse of the lake. This busy tourist centre has a wide range of attractions, from fishing trips to lake cruises, bungee-jumping and visits to geothermal areas. Covering over 600sq km at the geographical heart of the North Island, Lake Taupo is New Zealand's largest lake. This enormous, water-filled crater was formed by a series of massive eruptions which began around 250,000 years ago. Taupo's violent past is, however, masked by the tranquil lake waters which draw thousands of fishermen each year to what is claimed to be one of the best trout fisheries in the world.

Taupo's geothermal heritage is more evident in the thermal pools, such as **AC Baths**, just outside of town, which has several mineral pools and private spas. Similar facilities are available at the **Taupo Hot Springs**, hidden away in a wooded valley off the Taupo–Napier road.

Lounging around in hot pools is one way of using up geothermal heat, but at the Wairakei Geothermal Power Station it generates up to 1,100GWh (Giga watt hours) of power for the national grid. Completed in 1958, this was the second geothermal power station in the world

An attractive park on the shores of Lake Taupo

and you can see how 1,200 tonnes of steam per hour are captured at the **Wairakei Steamfield** just outside Taupo. There is a visitor centre at the entrance to the steamfield.

Other geothermal phenomena in the vicinity include the **Craters of the Moon** area, with its bubbling mud pools, and the **Wairakei Thermal Valley**, just past the steamfield.

Hot water is also put to good use at the **Wairakei Prawn Farm**, where you can round off a tour of the prawn ponds with a meal in the grillhouse afterwards. From the nearby landing stage a vintage riverboat, the ***African Queen***, cruises up the Waikato to the spectacular Huka Falls. A speedier way of getting there is on the ***Huka Jet***, or you can make your way on foot from the Huka Falls Road. Elsewhere along the river you can go rafting or jump off a 45m-high cantilever platform above the water at **Taupo Bungy**. There are plenty of options for lake cruises, most of which visit contemporary Maori rock-carvings on the lake's shore; the two most popular ships are the ***Barbary*** (a 1920s wooden racing yacht once owned by Errol Flynn) and the ***Ernest Kemp***, a replica steam ferry. Or if you prefer more modern transport,

Relaxing on the shores of Lake Taupo, New Zealand's largest lake

enjoy a cruise on the *Cruise Cat* catamaran, which offers daily sailings or can be privately chartered.

*AC Baths, Spa Road. Tel: 07 378 7321. Open: daily, 8am–9pm. Admission charge. Taupo Hot Springs, 1km along the Taupo–Napier highway. Tel: 07 378 8559. Open: daily 8am–9.30pm. Admission charge.*

*Wairakei Steamfield – open: 24 hours. Visitor Centre, Wairakei Road. Tel: 07 374 8216. Open: daily 9am–4.30pm. Free. Craters of the Moon, 5km north of Taupo. Open: dawn until dusk. Free. Wairakei Thermal Valley, Wairakei Park. Tel: 07 374 8004. Open: daily 8am–5pm. Admission charge. Wairakei Prawn Farm, Wairakei Park. Tel:*

*07 374 8303. Tours: daily, on the hour from 11am–4pm (summer); noon, 2 and 4pm (winter). Admission charge.*

The African Queen. *Tel: 07 374 8338. Departs: daily, 11am, 3pm, 6pm (9pm in summer).*

Huka Jet. *Tel: 07 374 8572. Departs: daily every half-hour. Taupo Bungy, Spa Road. Tel: 07 377 1135.*

The Barbary. *Tel: 07 378 3444. Departs: daily 10am and 2pm.*

The Ernest Kemp. *Tel: 07 378 6136. Departs: daily 10.30am and 2pm.*

Cruise Cat, *Lake Taupo Cruising Company, PO Box 1140. Tel: 07 378 1804.*

*84km south of Rotorua.*

## TONGARIRO NATIONAL PARK

Created in 1887, Tongariro was New Zealand's first national park. The three main peaks in Tongariro are Ruapehu (2,797m; the North Island's highest peak), Ngauruhoe (2,290m; its symmetrical cone is the most active of the three) and Tongariro itself (1,968; the oldest volcano). The first tourists began arriving in 1901, and in 1929 the famous Chateau Tongariro (one of New Zealand's best known hotels) was completed. Skiing began in the 1930s. All three volcanoes have erupted during this century; an early warning system and evacuation plans posted on hotel walls are a constant reminder of the unpredictability of this dramatic area.

The main access points to the park are Ohakune, Turangi and Whakapapa Village (leading from the settlement of National Park). Ohakune has the best selection of motels, restaurants and other amenities, while Turangi is handy for walking tracks in the northern section of the park. Chateau Tongariro and the main DOC visitor centre (with audio-visual displays on volcanic activity and the Maori heritage) are at Whakapapa Village. The National Park is primarily a service centre and stop on the main trunk railway line. There is excellent walking throughout the park, from short 30-minute rambles over volcanic features to the more demanding Round the Mountain Track; details available from the DOC centre.

*Whakapapa is 354km from Auckland, 341km from Wellington. DOC visitor centre, Whakapapa. Tel: 07 892 3729. Open: daily 8am–5pm.*

## WAITOMO CAVES

The Waitomo Caves are ranked as one of the great natural wonders of New Zealand, primarily thanks to the presence of a particular type of glow-worm (*Arachnocampa luminosa*). The larva of the glow-worm clings to cave roofs, spinning a delicate thread which it uses to ensnare insects that are attracted to its light. The main cave where they are found is the **Waitomo Cave**. Here, after the usual tour, you board a boat for a short trip down the underground river to the Glowworm Grotto. The effect is quite magical, with the thousands of glow-worms suspended on the cave roof above appearing like

Limestone formations in the Waitomo Cave

'Black-water rafting' is a popular way of exploring the caves for young visitors

twinkling stars on a clear night. In peak season 1,500 people descend daily into the Waitomo Cave, so try to come either early in the morning or late in the afternoon if you don't want to find yourself on a tourist conveyor belt.

The second main cave is the **Aranui**. It doesn't have glow-worms but it is still worth visiting for its delicate limestone formations. The third cave is **Ruakuri**, and at present the only way to see it is by black-water rafting, where you descend into the cave system and float along on your back, propelled by the current and supported by a rubber tyre. Ruakuri also has glow-worms, and there are plans to open it up to more general access to ease overcrowding in the main caves.

Just near the Waitomo Cave is the **Museum of Caves**, with audio-visual shows and displays about the glow-worms. On the road out to Waitomo it is worth stopping at the **Ohaki Maori Village**, a replica Maori village complete with *wharetohutohu* (nursery/learning houses), *wharepunis* (sleeping houses) and *pataka* (food-storage houses).

*Guided tours: Waitomo Cave, 9am–4.30pm (later in summer) every hour; Aranui Cave, 10am–3pm five times daily (more frequently in busy periods). Tickets for both must be bought at Waitomo Cave, Te Anga Road (tel: 07 878 8227).*
*Museum of Caves, Waitomo Cave Village. Tel: 07 878 7640. Open: daily 8.30am–5pm. Admission charge.*
*Ohaki Maori Village. Tel: 07 878 6610. Open: daily 10am–8pm. Admission charge.*
*Black-water Rafting, PO Box 13, Waitomo Cave. Tel: 07 878 6219. Waitomo Adventures Ltd, Waitomo Caves Road. Tel: 07 878 7788.*

*150km from Rotorua, signposted off the main Highway 3.*

# Coromandel

This route follows the beautiful west coast of the Coromandel Peninsula up to remote Fletcher Bay, where the road ends. It passes deserted beaches where you can stop for a swim, and runs alongside the peninsula's rugged, forested hills. The last section of the route (north of Colville) is along gravel roads, so if you have a hire car you may need to check insurance restrictions. *Allow a whole day, one way.*

*From Thames, follow the coast road (SH25) north to Tapu. Just past Tapu is Te Mata Beach.*

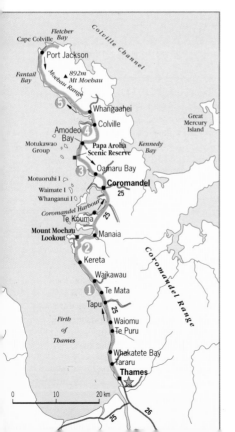

## 1 TE MATA BEACH

The Coromandel has yielded a wider variety of gemstones than anywhere else in the country, and Te Mata Beach is a particularly good place to look for large specimens of cornelian agate. Elsewhere, you might come across jasper, amethyst, chalcedony and petrified wood on the peninsula's beaches.

*Continue until the road climbs a bluff to the Mount Moehau look-out.*

## 2 MOUNT MOEHAU

Beneath you is the wide sweep of Coromandel Harbour, with the Moehau Range rising up ahead towards the middle of the peninsula. The highest point is Mount Moehau (892m); the mountain is a sacred Maori site and the burial place of Chief Tamatekapua, captain of the *Arawa*, one of the early canoes carrying immigrants from Hawaiki which arrived here around 1350. The range is also home to a rare native frog, *Leiopeima archeyi*, although you may well have to trek part of the way up Mount Moehau for the chance to spot this small, primeval creature.

A focal point for the community, the General Store is the only shop in Colville

*Descend into Coromandel (see page 56) and follow the signs for Colville.*

### 3 BEACHES AND BAYS
The road winds up over a hill before descending into Oamaru Bay (where there is a campsite), and then continues on to the Papa Aroha Scenic Reserve, a small area of native bush on the headland. A 20-minute amble through the reserve's typical coastal forest of *pohutukawa*, *puriri* and *kohekohe* takes you to a quiet little beach.
*Colville lies a further 12km from Papa Aroha.*

### 4 COLVILLE
Once a major centre for *kauri* milling, this small community on Colville Bay is now surrounded by farmland and arts and crafts communities. This is your last chance to stock up on picnic supplies or stop for refreshments before tackling the cape road.
*A short distance further on the road divides – take the left fork which is signposted to Port Jackson.*

### 5 THE CAPE ROAD
The road hugs the shoreline most of the way up the coast from here, passing between the gnarled, wind-shaped trunks of ancient *pohutukawa* trees; in summer these are a magnificent sight, their bright red blossoms hanging from boughs over the beaches and rocks. Passing the campsite at Fantail Bay, the road becomes more and more tricky (not for nothing is this known as one of the most hair-raising roads in North Island) but the views become increasingly spectacular until, just after the big beach at Port Jackson, you finally arrive at the end of the road in Fletcher Bay. This lovely cove is shaded by *pohutukawa* trees and there is a campsite, good fishing and, if you are feeling energetic, the option of a short hike over the headland to the 150m-high Needles.
*Return to Coromandel along the same road.*

# Wellington and Taranaki

*T*he Taranaki region, on the west coast of the North Island, is dominated by the snow-capped peak of Mount Taranaki/Egmont itself. The eruptions of this now-dormant volcano have covered the surrounding lands with fertile ash. This and the high rainfall on Taranaki's slopes have created lush pastures, put to good use by the numerous local dairy herds which produce some of the country's finest cheeses. This region has not always been so peaceful, for it was here that the Land Wars of the 1860s between *pakeha* and Maori erupted, and some of the bloodiest engagements took place in these surroundings.

From Taranaki's upper slopes there are sweeping panoramas across to the fuming cones of the Tongariro National Park and out along the coastline. On the mountain's north side, the city of New Plymouth spreads along the coast, its vast offshore reserves of natural gas creating energy for the national grid. The city is also renowned for its extensive displays of rhododendrons and azaleas, and surfies and board-sailers are drawn to the rolling breakers that crash in off the Tasman Sea on to the beaches near by.

Heading south from Taranaki you soon come to the mighty Wanganui river, the longest navigable river in the country. Steamers, jet-boats and other assorted craft offer rides upstream from the riverside city of Wanganui, which also has a good museum and art galleries. Inland lies Palmerston North, a thriving agricultural centre forming the crossroads between Taranaki, Wellington and central North Island.

If you cross the Tararua Range eastwards from Palmerston North, you reach the rolling plains which descend to the Pacific Ocean. These form the dairy and sheep pastures of the Wairarapa, with the regional centre, Masterton, playing host to the annual 'Golden Shears' international sheep-shearing competition. In contrast to the untold numbers of sheep surrounding them, just a handful of some of the rarest and most endangered bird species in the country are nurtured and protected at the Mount Bruce National

Martinborough is well known for its vineyards

# WELLINGTON AND TARANAKI

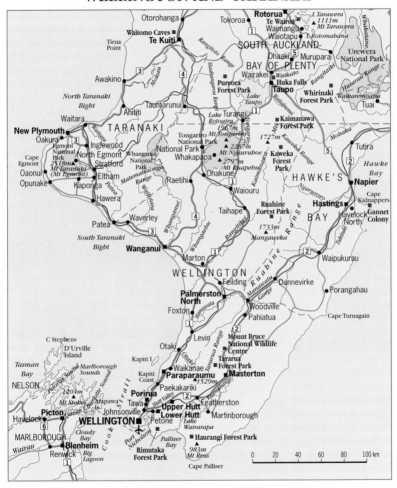

Wildlife Centre, just north of Masterton, a must for wildlife enthusiasts.

South of Masterton, the vineyards of Martinborough are fast gaining a reputation for their fine wines, whilst eastwards the sea beats mercilessly on the rugged, inhospitable Wairarapa coastline. Heading south again across the Rimutaka Range, you reach the dormitory cities of Upper Hutt and Lower Hutt. These eventually merge into the outskirts of Wellington, the nation's capital, set amidst steep hills that overlook its vast harbour.

## MOUNT BRUCE NATIONAL WILDLIFE CENTRE

The National Wildlife Centre consists of numerous aviaries built around native bush on the slopes of Mount Bruce, and plays a crucial role in ensuring the survival of some of the most threatened and endangered species in New Zealand. The centre was established in 1958 to attempt captive breeding of the *takahe*, a bird which was thought to be extinct until the dramatic discovery of a small colony in Fiordland in 1948. Today, the centre offers the opportunity for visitors to see some of the rarest species in the world, many of which cannot be seen anywhere else since they only survive on offshore islands.

As well as the *takahe* (of which there are currently only around 200 left), other species you may spot include *kokako*, saddlebacks and stitchbirds from the bush, rare black stilts from wetland areas and the nocturnal morepork forest owl. The centre has the largest nocturnal house in the country, where brown kiwis have been bred successfully for the last 30 years; breeding programmes have now

The Mount Bruce National Wildlife Centre is well worth visiting to see rare and endangered birds

also started for the great spotted and little spotted kiwis. The centre also has heated burrows with one-way windows to maximise your chances of seeing the elusive and rare lizard-like *tuatara* (see page 15).

Currently, the work of the centre is focused on six priority species: the Campbell and Auckland Islands' teals, the New Zealand pigeon, the shore plover, the saddleback, the stitchbird and the *kokako*. The latter is one of the most endangered species in the world, with only eight known breeding females alive today.

*30km north of Masterton on SH2. National Wildlife Centre, Mount Bruce. Tel: 06 375 8004. Open: daily 8.30am–4pm. Admission charge.*

## MOUNT TARANAKI/EGMONT

Dominating the surrounding dairyland for miles around, the solitary peak of Mount Taranaki rises up on North Island's west coast like a lonely sentinel. Because it adjoins the sea, it even has its own weather system and is often shrouded in cloud – Abel Tasman, sailing by in 1642, missed it altogether and it was left to Captain Cook to name

it when he sighted the peak in 1770. Cook called it Mount Egmont (after the Earl of Egmont, then First Lord of the Admiralty) and, although it has since reverted to its Maori name of Taranaki, it now goes under the joint name of Mt Taranaki/Egmont. The surrounding national park is still known as Egmont National Park.

The mountain is rich in Maori mythology and legend. Taranaki has always been held as *tapu* (sacred) by the Maori, who used to travel up the surrounding river valleys to collect red ochre and bury the bones of their chiefs and *tohungas* (priests) in secret caves on its slopes.

Taranaki is an unpredictable mountain, sunny and clear one minute, treacherous and windswept the next. Many climbers have lost their lives here, but despite this it is still one of the country's most frequently climbed peaks – largely thanks to the local alpine club's open invitation climbs which have seen up to 600 people reach the summit in a day. On a clear day there are magnificent views from the summit across to Tongariro and out over the Tasman Sea. The peak can be climbed in a single day, but always consult park staff as to conditions.

The main visitor centre is at North Egmont, where there is a comprehensive exhibition centre and details on the mountain huts and routes. Even if you are not attempting a major climb, it is well worth the effort driving out here on a fine day and taking one of the marked trails which lead through the surrounding *kamihi* and *totara* forest.

*North Egmont Visitor Centre, Egmont Road, 26km from New Plymouth, signposted off Highway 3. Tel: 06 756 8710. Open: daily 8.30am–4.30pm in summer, closed Monday and Tuesday in winter.*

A bust of Sir Harry Atkinson at Hurworth Cottage, outside New Plymouth

formal, European-style gardens, as does the 3.6-hectare **Tupare Gardens**. A half-hour drive out of the city takes you to the **Pukeiti Rhododendron Trust**, with its brilliant displays of rhododendrons and azaleas between September and November. On the way to Pukeiti you can also visit **Hurworth**, a historic pioneer cottage built by an immigrant, Harry Atkinson, who later became premier of New Zealand for four terms of office.

New Plymouth is a convenient base for visiting Mount Egmont, Taranaki (see page 79), and as well as some excellent surfing and windsurfing beaches it also has a seal colony in the **Sugar Loaf Marine Park**, just past the power station.

*The main entrance to Pukekura Park and Brooklands is on Fillis Street, 10 minutes' walk from the city centre. Open: daily 9am–5pm. Free.*

*Tupare Gardens, Mangorei Road. Open: daily September to March 9am–5pm; April to August, open by arrangement. Admission charge.*

*Pukeiti Rhododendron Trust, Carrington Road. Open: daily 9am–5pm. Admission charge.*

*Hurworth Cottage, 522 Carrington Road. Tel: 06 753 6545. Open: Wednesday to Sunday 10am–4pm. Admission charge. Seal colony trips are organised by Chaddy's Charters (tel: 06 758 9133).*

*180km southwest of Waitomo, 164km northwest of Wanganui.*

## NEW PLYMOUTH

Lying midway between Auckland and Wellington on the west coast, the city of New Plymouth is an important energy-production centre. Oil drilling began here as early as 1865, but this was eclipsed by the discovery of vast reserves of natural gas in the offshore Kapuni field in 1962 and the Maui field in 1969.

Beautification programmes have turned New Plymouth into an attractive city with a plethora of lovely parks and gardens within the city centre. The most well known of these is **Pukekura Park**, which features a lovely combination of lakes and streams, rolling lawns, native and exotic trees, fern gullies and flowers. Neighbouring **Brooklands** has more

## WANGANUI

This bustling, lively city lies at the mouth of New Zealand's longest navigable river and, from the time of the earliest Maori settlements, it has been an important supply route to the interior. Nowadays, it is not canoes but jet-boats and paddle-steamers that carry passengers upstream on scenic trips.

Running through the heart of Wanganui down to the river is Victoria Avenue; most of the city's attractions lie within a few minutes' walk of this busy shopping thoroughfare. Just off Victoria Avenue is the **Wanganui Regional Museum**, possibly the largest regional museum in the country. It has an excellent collection of artefacts in its Maori Court; pride of place goes to the historic war canoe *Te Mata-O-Hoturoa*, which saw action in the 1870s (bullets are still embedded in its hull). The museum also houses the skeleton of a giant moa and colonial artefacts.

Just behind the museum is the **Sarjeant Art Gallery**, with a major collection of New Zealand and British works from the 19th and early 20th centuries, as well as contemporary art.

Wanganui has numerous parks (including a deer park, Virginia Lake Scenic Reserve and Riverland Family Park), an interesting church with Maori carvings at Putiki (St Paul's), and a hideous tower on Durie Hill (on the opposite side of the riverbank), with sweeping views of the town and river mouth.

*Regional Museum, Maria Place. Tel: 06 345 7443. Open: Monday to Saturday 10am–4pm, Sunday 1–4.30pm. Admission charge. Sarjeant Art Gallery, Queen's Park. Tel: 06 345 8529. Open: weekdays 10.30am–4.30pm, weekends 1–4.30pm. Details on parks, other attractions and river trips are available from the Wanganui Information Centre, 101 Guyton Street. Tel: 06 345 3286. Open: weekday 8.30am–5pm, weekends 10am–2pm.*

*193km north of Wellington.*

Pukekura Park is one of many beautiful gardens in the city of New Plymouth

# Wellington

*M*aori legend has it that the explorer Kupe was the first to discover Wellington's harbour. When the first Europeans arrived in 1840 the Maoris welcomed them, hoping that they would provide protection against hostile neighbouring tribes.

Wellington was the first of several settlements set up by the London-based New Zealand Company and quickly became a successful trading post. Although Governor Hobson initially chose Auckland as his capital, it was too far away from the rapidly increasing population of the South Island and a commission eventually chose Wellington as the new capital in 1865.

As the administrative capital and a rapidly growing business centre, the city's main disadvantage was the lack of flat land for building, so land reclamation (helped along by a huge earthquake which partially raised the sea bed in 1855) began in the harbour, a process that continues today. Squeezed in by the hills that surround it, Wellington is thus a very compact city and, unlike Auckland, easy to get around on foot. The lack of space means that many workers commute in from outlying suburbs and cities, such as Porirua and Lower and Upper Hutt to the north.

Dubbed the 'windy city', Wellington is noted for the winds that can whistle through the Cook Strait. These can reach speeds of 90kph and are funnelled by the high-rise blocks into a fearsome maelstrom in the city centre. Blowing mostly in the spring and autumn, these enervating winds are, on the positive side, credited with blowing away any smog and putting backbone into the Wellingtonian character!

Whilst Wellington remains at heart a city of government bureaucrats, diplomats and international business, it is also striving to create a role for itself as the events and cultural capital of the country. The city is home to the Museum of New Zealand, four professional theatre companies, the New Zealand Symphony Orchestra and the Royal New Zealand Ballet, and hosts the biennial New Zealand International Festival of the Arts – just one of numerous festivals that take place here each year. An ever-expanding range of nightspots, cafés and restaurants has also added to the vibrancy of the capital in recent years.

At the heart of Wellington's renaissance are the massive improvements to Lambton Harbour, just a few steps from the core business and shopping area along

High-rise blocks crowd the waterfront in New Zealand's capital

Lambton Quay. Old wharf buildings and sheds have been imaginatively renovated and the star attraction of the development is the Museum of New Zealand (Te Papa Tongarewa) which opened early 1998. Housed in a huge purpose-built building, the museum covers every aspect of New Zealand's land, life and loves and will take at least a morning to browse around. The country's capital also offers Frank Kitt's Park, Lagoon Beach (featuring water sculptures and boardwalks), dockside restaurants, apartments and shops, and a new marina.

# WELLINGTON

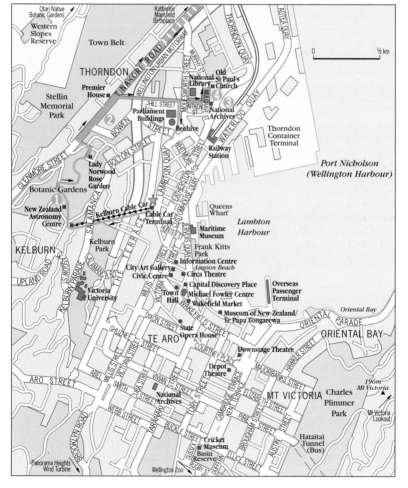

## BOTANIC GARDENS

See page 88.

## CAPITAL DISCOVERY PLACE/TE AHO A MAUI

An excellent children's science museum where even adults will have fun. The exhibits, nearly all of which are interactive, focus on robots, virtual reality, the environment, body senses and so on. There is also a special section for the under-fives and a three-dimensional maze. *Te Aho A Maui* means 'Line of Maui', referring to the legend of Maui hooking the North Island on his fishing line. This symbolic line is a theme throughout the building, reflecting the idea (according to the brochure) of 'moving beyond conventional Western frameworks to incorporate Maori and Polynesian values into a holistic approach to learning'.
*Civic Square. Tel: 04 801 3980 – information line. Open: Tuesday to Sunday 10am–5pm. Admission charge.*

## CITY ART GALLERY

Since 1993 the City Art Gallery has been housed in the former Public Library overlooking Civic Square, a cavernous building where there is ample space for the many stimulating exhibitions put on here each year. The programme covers art, architecture, design, photography and the moving image, and exhibitions are usually of a very high standard. With at least three or four main exhibitions running at any one time, it is always worth looking in to see what's on.
*Civic Square. Tel: 04 801 3952. Open: weekdays 11am–5pm, weekends, 11am–6pm winter (Thursdays until 8pm all year). Free.*

## CRICKET MUSEUM

A cricket bat dating from 1743 (one of the three oldest in existence) is just one of the hundreds of items of New Zealand and international memorabilia, ancient and modern, on display here.
*The Old Grandstand, Basin Reserve Grounds, Buckle and Sussex streets. Open: daily 10.30am–3.30pm summer; all day on match days April to October only. Admission charge.*

## KATHERINE MANSFIELD BIRTHPLACE

Born in an unassuming-looking two-storey wooden house in 1888, Katherine Mansfield later became one of the world's best-known short-story writers and New Zealand's most famous author. Although Mansfield left the country when she was 19, many of her best stories (such as *Prelude, The Aloe* and *A Birthday*) were based on her childhood memories of this house.

The house has been carefully restored and furnished with period antiques – even the wallpaper has been re-created from fragments found here. Photographs, videos and tapes evoke Mansfield's short but eventful life, and the notes which you will be given on entry link the different rooms and settings to events in her stories. The garden has also been set out in its original Victorian design.
*25 Tinakori Road, Thorndon, 10 minutes' walk from the railway station. Tel: 04 473 7268. Open: Monday 10am–2.30pm, Tuesday to Sunday 10am–4pm. Admission charge.*

A trip on Wellington's cable-car is a good way to gain an overview of the city

### KELBURN CABLE CAR

Built in 1902, the cable car (now with modern Swiss cars) glides upwards past Victoria University of Wellington for a five-minute ride to Kelburn suburb and the Botanic Gardens (see page 88).
*Cable Car Lane, off Lambton Quay. Open: weekdays 7am–10pm, weekends 9am–6pm. Single or return fares.*

### MARITIME MUSEUM

Until refurbishment is completed, the museum's exhibits are housed in a building near by. These include displays of model ships, brass telescopes, ships'

bells and the like, but there are also one or two surprises which make it well worth a visit: an evocative display on the sinking of the *Wahine*, a passenger ferry which foundered in Wellington Harbour in 1968 with the loss of 51 lives, and an interactive computer simulation of an oil spill, in which you have to make the decisions about how to deal with it to save a fragile coastal environment.
*Queens Wharf, City. Tel: 04 472 8904. Open: weekdays 9.30am–4pm, weekends 10am–4.30pm (April to November, weekdays 9.30am–4pm, weekends 1–5pm). Donation.*

Wellington Zoo has an active conservation and breeding programme for endangered species

## MOUNT VICTORIA LOOKOUT

The Maori name for this hill on the southeastern edge of the harbour basin was Matai-rangi, which means 'To Watch the Sky', indicating that it was probably once used as a look-out point. The panorama of the city and harbour from here has been somewhat superseded by the opening of the road up to the Panorama Heights Wind Turbine (see opposite).

*Mount Victoria is signposted from Oriental Bay and Courtenay Place and can also be reached via Constable Street and Alexandra Road. Otherwise, take bus 20 (Monday to Friday) from the railway station.*

## MUSEUM OF NEW ZEALAND/ TE PAPA TONGAREWA

Magnificently situated in its new, purpose-built home on the stunning Wellington waterfront, Te Papa is a gateway for visitors to discover and understand the rich history of New Zealand. This exciting museum allows visitors to travel through time to visit New Zealand in the past and future, using a combination of displays and leading-edge technology. See how earthquakes, cyclones and volcanoes have shaped the landscape. Experience the eruptions of Mount Ruapehu. Discover how New Zealand's native plants and animals, many of them unique, have adapted to their environments. Uncover a dinosaur and explore some of the oldest rock formations in the country.

On a spectacular platform, high above the harbour is Te Marae, a fully functioning *marae* and its focal point, Te Hono ki Hawaiki, a *wharenui* (meeting house).

*Cable Street. Tel: 04 381 7000. Open: daily 10am–6pm; Thursday until 9pm. Free.*

## NATIONAL ARCHIVES

See page 89.

## OLD ST PAUL'S CHURCH

See page 89.

## OTARI NATIVE BOTANIC GARDENS

This 80-hectare park is a sanctuary entirely devoted to the cultivation and preservation of indigenous plants, and contains the largest such collection in the country. There are over 10km of walking tracks, picnic areas and rock gardens, plus an information centre. The gardens are also rich in native bird life; you may

see tuis, fantails, grey warblers and kingfishers flitting from tree to tree.
*Wilton Road, Wadestown. 20 minutes' from the city centre on bus 14. Tel: 04 473 3245. Open: daily dawn to dusk; information centre open: weekdays only 8am–4pm. Free.*

## PANORAMA HEIGHTS WIND TURBINE

Opened in 1993, this massive 31m-high wind turbine generator is part of an experiment to see whether the 'windy city' really is windy enough to generate its own electricity. The graceful, Danish-designed turbine can generate up to 225kW – enough to power around 120 homes – on a blustery day. Information boards (with a digital read-out of the energy being generated) are next to the car-park at the top. There are fabulous views from the top – even Mount Victoria looks like a mere molehill way below in the distance.
*Panorama Heights Wind Turbine. Sign-posted off Brooklyn Road, commences at the end of Willis Street, about 20 minutes' drive from downtown. Access road open: daily 8am–8pm summer, 8am–5pm winter. Free. For further information, contact Electricity New Zealand (ECNZ), PO Box 930, Wellington.*

## PARLIAMENT BUILDINGS

The old Parliament Building, which once laid claim to being the largest all-wood building in the world, burned down in 1907 and was replaced with the current Italianate-style building which houses the two debating chambers; it has recently undergone extensive renovation to make it earthquake proof. Next door is the unmistakable Beehive (which houses the executive wing of government), designed by Sir Basil Spence and completed in 1981. You can tour the Parliament

Building and visit the Public Gallery in the debating chamber.
*Lambton Quay. Free guided tours. Tel: 04 719 999 for times.*

## WELLINGTON ZOO

Native flora and fauna, as well as more exotic wildlife, are on display. Kiwis can be seen in the Nocturnal House daily, 10am–4pm.
*Manchester Street, Newton. 4km from the city centre; bus 10 from the railway station. Tel: 04 389 8130. Open: daily 9.30am–5pm. Admission charge.*

The 'windy city' generates power from this experimental turbine on Panorama Heights

# Wellington

This walk encompasses several of the more interesting historic sights in Wellington's centre, as well as the extensive Botanic Gardens. It is an easy walk, largely because the cable-car takes you to the top of the hill – after that it is a continuous descent. For route see map on page 83. *Allow around 2 hours (plus time to visit Katherine Mansfield's birthplace, see Thorndon).*

*Start at Kelburn Cable Car terminal on Lambton Quay (see page 85). Turn right immediately into the Botanic Gardens.*

## 1 BOTANIC GARDENS

The 25-hectare gardens have more than the usual variety of plantings, ranging from native bush to herb gardens, exotic fern gardens and a circular rose garden. At the summit of the hill is the New Zealand Astronomy Centre, which has a planetarium, astronomy displays and hands-on computer programs. Wander down the hill, passing the Education and Environment Centre and ending up at the Lady Norwood Rose Garden at the bottom and leaving via the Centennial Entrance on the north side. *Turn right and walk down Tinakori Road.*

## 2 THORNDON

Tinakori Road is the main artery of Thorndon, a suburb where the first Europeans settled in the 1840s. There are some charming old wooden houses on either side, many now converted into up-market shops, bistros and cafés. Just past the junction with Upton Terrace is Premier House, which served as the Prime Minister's residence from 1875 until 1937 and

Wellington's Botanic Gardens offer a respite from the bustle of the city

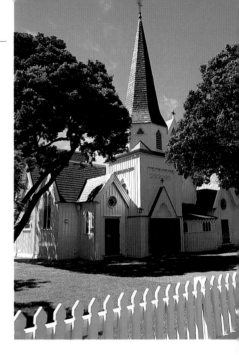

Old St Paul's is a delightful wooden building in the heart of modern Wellington

is once again the official residence of the Prime Minister.

*You can continue to the bottom of Tinakori Road to visit Katherine Mansfield's Birthplace (see page 84); allow an extra 40 minutes to see the house and return to the Hill Street turn-off. Turn right down Hill Street and continue to the junction with Mulgrave Street. Directly opposite is the National Archives building.*

## *3* NATIONAL ARCHIVES

Inside the National Archives, turn right for the air-conditioned vault where the Treaty of Waitingi and several dozen other important historical documents are stored. The Treaty itself looks rather torn and battered (it travelled around the country for several months until the 213 signatures necessary for its implementation were collected), but it is the genuine article.

*Turn right out of the National Archives to Old St Paul's Church.*

## *4* OLD ST PAUL'S CHURCH

Designed by parish vicar and architect Rev Frederick Thatcher in 1866, this all-wood church was built entirely using native timbers and is a marvellous example of the Gothic Revival style adapted to wood. The soft lighting and dark timber of the panelling, pews and soaring arches exude a sense of warmth and serenity alongside numerous brass plaques in honour of local parishioners. This lovely church was scheduled for demolition to make way for a new cathedral, but in 1966 it was given over to the Historic Places Trust. Today it is used for music and drama events and special services.

*Go back down Aitken Street (opposite the National Archives) and through the courtyard in front of Parliament Buildings and the Beehive (see page 87), crossing Bowen Street to return to Lambton Quay.*

**Botanic Gardens** (tel: 04 473 0698). Open: daily dawn–dusk. Free.
**New Zealand Astronomy Centre** (tel: 04 472 8167). Open: weekdays 10am–5pm, weekends noon–5pm. Continuous shows 12.15–4.15pm weekends. Admission charge.
**Planetarium shows:** weekends and school holidays, 10.15am–4.15pm.
**National Archives,** 10 Mulgrave Street (tel: 04 499 5595). Open: weekdays 9am–5pm, Saturdays 9am–1pm. Free.
**Old St Paul's,** Mulgrave Street (tel: 04 473 6722). Open: Monday to Saturday 10am–5pm.

# Nelson and Marlborough

*I*t doesn't take long to cross the often turbulent Cook Strait on the inter-island ferries from Wellington to the South Island, but, once you pass the first headland and start steaming down what looks like a fiord, there is still an hour's journey ahead before you reach the port of Picton. This massive inlet is part of the Marlborough Sounds (despite appearances, it is a sunken valley rather than a fiord), and its myriad inlets, bays and wooded coves make it a popular holiday area. Boat transport is *de rigueur* here as roads are few and far between, and if you want to go hiking, fishing, bird-watching or camping there are plenty of launches and speedboats to ferry you to isolated spots within the Marlborough Sounds Maritime Park.

At the head of Queen Charlotte Sound is Picton, the gateway to the South Island for ferry passengers. If you have time on your hands, the surrounding scenery is best appreciated by hiking the Queen Charlotte Walkway; alternatively, an hour's drive or so around the coastline on the Queen Charlotte Drive to Havelock provides wonderful views of this beautiful area.

South of Picton lies Blenheim, the administrative centre of the Marlborough region and, thanks to its high sunshine record, the centre of a flourishing wine industry. Marlborough's benevolent climate is partly due to the protection offered by the Kaikoura Mountains to the south and east. The coastal town of Kaikoura, on the other side of this range, has become a magnet for ecotourism thanks to the year-round presence of mighty sperm whales, not to mention dolphins, fur seals and other marine life.

Protecting Marlborough on its western flank, the Richmond Range marks the boundary with the neighbouring region of Nelson. Horticulture and fruit-growing thrive in Nelson's equally balmy climate, and its glacial valleys, forest parks and rushing rivers form the backdrop to numerous

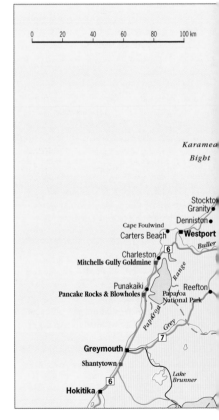

outdoor activities. Nelson city is the focal point of the region; the many sheltered bays and beaches near by are popular for family camping holidays. To the south, the twin lakes of Rotoroa and Rotoiti sit high up in the Nelson Lakes National Park, surrounded by forests which are criss-crossed with walking and hiking tracks. Hunting and fishing opportunities abound.

West of Nelson, the highway skirts Tasman Bay before climbing steeply over Takaka Hill to descend into Golden Bay. The last sleepy outposts in this remote corner of the South Island come alive in the summer months as people flock to the beaches and the sea, or pause briefly before setting off on famous trails such as the Heaphy Track and the Abel Tasman Coastal Walk. Curving around the top of Golden Bay, Farewell Spit is a 30km-long sand bar (mostly accessed on 4WD tours) where thousands of wading and wetland birds nest in the summer months.

# NELSON AND MARLBOROUGH

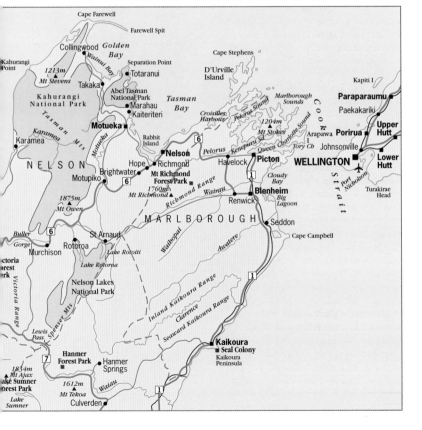

The mild climate in the Wairau Plain has led to the growth of numerous vineyards around Blenheim

## ABEL TASMAN NATIONAL PARK

This is one of the smallest national parks in New Zealand; it covers just 22,350 hectares and was named in honour of Abel Tasman on 19 December, 1942, the 300th anniversary of his visit. In fact, Tasman's landfall here wasn't a happy one: his canoes were attacked by the local Maori, four men were killed, and he left quickly. The French explorer Dumont d'Urville had better luck in January, 1827 and, having befriended the locals, charted the coastline here. Permanent European settlers arrived during the 1850s, logging the forests and quarrying for granite. Shipwrights also moved in, taking advantage of the protected bay and fine timber. Logging came to a halt after a vigorous campaign spearheaded by a local woman, Perrine Moncrieff, who persuaded the government to create the park in 1942.

Despite its small size, Abel Tasman is one of the most popular national parks in the country with hikers. The coastal track follows a succession of beautiful clean beaches and shimmering bays backed by rolling hillsides of rain forest thick with nikau palms, vines, perching plants and tree ferns. An alternative inland route passes through magnificent beech forests. An added bonus is that the tracks are easy and accessible: there are no mountainous gradients on the coastal section and scheduled boat services even hop between the bays to drop off and pick up day-trippers and backpackers.

The three main access points to the park are at Marahau, Totaranui and Wainui Bay. Marahau lies just north of

Motueka (see page 98), while Wainui Bay lies 21km from Takaka (see Golden Bay, pages 94–5) and Totaranui lies 12km further on (this last section is on a narrow, unsealed road). For day walks, Totaranui and Marahau are the best bets (see page 148–9 for more details on the track).

*Details on day trips can be obtained from local DOC offices at Motueka (PO Box 97; tel: 03 528 9117) or Takaka (PO Box 53; tel: 03 525 9061). From Motueka, Abel Tasman Seafaris (tel: 03 527 8083) depart daily at 9am heading northwards to Awaroa Bay; from Tarakohe Harbour (just north of Takaka) The* Spirit of Golden Bay *(tel: 03 525 9153) departs daily at 9am and drops passengers off at 10 different bays before continuing all the way to Nelson; the return trip departs from Nelson at 2.15pm.*

**BLENHEIM**

This busy provincial centre, the largest town in the Marlborough region, is situated at the confluence of the Taylor and Opawa rivers amidst the flatlands of the Wairau Plain. The region has an enviable sunshine record, which prompted the setting up of the Montana vineyards here in the late 1960s; Blenheim is now the centre of a flourishing wine industry.

This neatly laid out town is renowned for its gardens, such as Pollard Park (just off Parker Street), which covers 25 hectares around the spring-fed Fulton Creek. There are rock gardens and

herbaceous borders to admire, as well as a fitness trail and children's playground. Seymour Square, in the town centre, is an attractive mix of lawns, specimen trees and floral displays.

The town's main historical interest lies in the **Brayshaw Historic Museum Park**, which has an extensive collection of vintage farm machinery, a mock colonial village and a miniature railway. *Both gardens are open during daylight hours.*

*Brayshaw Historic Museum Park, New Renwick Road. Tel: 03 578 1712. Open: Tuesday to Sunday 1–4pm. Admission charge.*

*These times may vary as the museum is fairly casual about opening times and may close or stay open longer depending on number of visitors on any particular day.*

*28km south of Picton, 132km north of Kaikoura.*

A blaze of colour in one of Blenheim's many gardens

## GOLDEN BAY

Golden Bay lies at the mouth of the Takaka river valley and is reached by a tortuous mountain road over Takaka Hill from Motueka. Like the Coromandel, Golden Bay became something of an 'alternative lifestyle' centre in the 1970s thanks to the availability of cheap smallholdings; today it is mostly known for its safe swimming beaches (with good windsurfing) and for the intensive dairy farming in the valley. Golden Bay is also one of the main access points for the coastal track through the Abel Tasman National Park (see pages 92–3).

The main centre for Golden Bay is the small township of **Takaka**. On the main street are the information centre, the DOC office and the **Takaka Museum**. The museum documents Tasman's arrival in the bay and has the usual collection of early settlers' mementoes, as well as shells, minerals and a few Maori artefacts.

Just outside Takaka, **Pupu Springs** (an abbreviation of the Maori name, Waikoropupu) are the largest freshwater springs in New Zealand. Water from the upper river valley disappears down into a huge underground cave system and emerges here at the rate of around 21cu m per second. There are at least 16 springs in the vicinity, with the two main springs visible from a platform located a short walk from the car-park.

North of Takaka is the even smaller community of **Collingwood**, first settled during the 1850s gold boom. Visitors to Collingwood today (with its one general store, hotel, garage and café) will find it hard to believe that at one time there was even a proposal to make it the capital of the country. If you have time to spare you can join the 'Mail Run', a five-hour scenic ride on the rural mail bus which

The tiny port of Havelock in Pelorus Sound

drops off post and supplies at isolated farms and communities. There is a running commentary on points of interest from the driver.

Beyond Collingwood is **Farewell Spit**, a 26km-long sand bar which acts as a breakwater for Golden Bay. The 20m-high sand dunes form an internationally renowned bird sanctuary, with over 90 species having been recorded here. Hundreds of thousands of migratory waders spend the summer here, including large flocks of bar-tailed godwits (up to 20,000) and knots (up to 30,000), as well as turnstones, long-billed curlews and many others. There are also large numbers of gulls, gannets, cormorants and other sea birds. Access to this important site is strictly controlled.

*The information centre (tel: 03 525 9136) is at the southern entrance to town.*

*Takaka Museum and Gallery, Commercial Street. Open: daily 10am–4pm. Admission charge.*

*Pupu Springs are 5km north of town, signposted off the SH60.*

Collingwood lies 28km from Takaka on the SH60.

The Mail Run leaves Monday to Friday at 9.30am (bookings through Collingwood Bus Service, Post Office, PO Box 61, Collingwood; tel: 03 524 8188).

Public access to Farewell Spit is restricted to a small area at the base of the spit unless with a licenced operator such as Farewell Spit Safaris (Tasman Street, PO Box 15, Collingwood; tel: 03 524 8257) or the Collingwood Bus Service (see above).

Takaka lies 57km from Motueka on SH60.

## HAVELOCK

Havelock lies half-way between Picton and Nelson, and stands at the head of Pelorus Sound, the largest of the Marlborough Sounds. The town is the main landing point for the tasty green-lipped mussels which are grown on ropes suspended in Marlborough Sounds and brought here for processing and export. Scallops are another local delicacy, and if you want to catch your own fish there are plenty of small boats for hire at the wharf.

70km west of Picton, 76km east of Nelson.

## KAIKOURA

The small seaside town of Kaikoura curves around an attractive bay, with the snow-capped peaks of the Kaikoura Mountains rising up behind it. This former whaling port is now enjoying a huge boom in ecotourism as people flock here to watch the sperm whales, seals and dolphins that abound in the offshore waters and around the rocky coastline of the peninsula.

Kaikoura has always been known for its sea life: the Maori came here for the same reason and christened the spot *kai* (meaning 'food' or 'to eat') *koura* (meaning 'crayfish').

Whaling began here in 1842. The only building still standing from this era is **Fyffe House** (1860), the residence of George Fyffe, one of the original whaling masters. The piles of his weatherboard cottage are giant whale vertebrae; the house is gradually being restored by the Historic Places Trust. Other reminders of whaling days are on show in the **Kaikoura Museum**, which also displays various local mementoes and a 1910 police lock-up (complete with padded cell).

Just outside the town is **Maori Leap Cave**. Discovered in 1958, the 90m-long sea cave is known for its delicate cave straws, tubular formations that grow at the rate of about 25mm every hundred years.

Other activities in and around Kaikoura include fishing, diving, swimming and snorkelling with seals and dolphins, or exploring the scenic Kaikoura Peninsula Walkway (see pages 100–1).

The **Kaikoura Visitor Centre** has an excellent audio-visual theatre which features spectacular multimedia presentations on the whales, dolphins, seals and seabirds. Shows are on the hour, daily, and there is an admission charge.

*Fyffe House, 62 Avoca Street. Open: daily 10am–4pm. Admission charge.*
*Kaikoura Museum, Ludstone Road. Open: daily 2–4pm. Admission charge.*
*Maori Leap Cave, 3km south on the SH1 behind the Caves Restaurant. Tel: 03 319 5023. Conducted tours six times daily. Admission charge.*
*Information centre, Esplanade. Tel: 03 319 5641. Open: daily.*

*132km south of Blenheim.*

The seaside town of Kaikoura on the South Island's east coast

# Whale and Dolphin Watching

*M*arine mammals abound in the waters around New Zealand but there are few places in such a fortunate position as Kaikoura when it comes to close-up viewing. Kaikoura's abundant marine resources are due to two phenomenon. First, nutrient-rich subantarctic waters meet subtropical waters here, resulting in an abundance of microscopic phytoplankton which form the basis of a complex food chain. Second, the sea-bed drops away nearly 1,000m into the Kaikoura Canyon, a mere 1km from the coast, which means that deep-water feeders such as sperm whales surface in these coastal waters alongside the dolphins and seals.

Although the sperm whales are the main attraction, you may also spot the tiny Hector's dolphin (the world's rarest dolphin), bottlenose and dusky dolphins, orcas and pilot whales, and sea birds including albatross, petrels and shearwaters.

The whale-watching boats use hydrophones (underwater microphones) to locate

Tourists watch a sperm whale dive down to the depths off Kaikoura

the distinctive clicking of the sperm whale. A tell-tale plume from the whale's blowhole pinpoints the spot where it has surfaced, and where it will remain for 10–12 minutes while it replenishes its oxygen supply before diving again. At this point the whales raise their massive tail flukes above the surface before disappearing from sight.

It is rare to see a sperm whale 'breach' (leap into the air) in the way humpbacks do, and only a small proportion of the resting whale is visible on the surface until it starts to dive. For some, this is frustrating, but for others it is privilege enough to be so close to this once-threatened creature.

Whale Watch Kaikoura operates four boats with four tours daily, 6am–2pm, each lasting 2½ hours. Advance reservations are advisable; allow more than one day in case ocean conditions force cancellations. *Whale Watch Kaikoura Ltd, the Whaleway Station, PO Box 89, Kaikoura (tel: 03 319 6767). Tours: adults, NZ$95; children, NZ$60.*

## MOTUEKA

Motueka is a busy base for trekkers and day-trippers setting off to the Abel Tasman National Park (see pages 92–3), and also for seasonal workers who arrive in the autumn. Motueka has a range of accommodation, plus shops for stocking up on supplies if you are tramping.

*51km northwest of Nelson, reached via Highway 6 and then Highway 60.*

## NELSON

Nelson is a bright and breezy city humming with activity – particularly arts and crafts as many potters have been drawn here by the availability of good local clay. You can explore Nelson's numerous galleries and workshops with the 'Arts Trail and Gallery Guide' leaflet (available from the information centre) or by taking an Arts Trail Guided Walk. A good place to browse is at **Craft Habitat**, with its ceramics, stained-glass, weaving and

jewellery workshops. Crafts are also often on display alongside a fine collection of early colonial oils and water-colours in the **Suter Art Gallery**.

Nelson's **Christ Church Cathedral** stands at the end of the main thoroughfare, Trafalgar Street. Colonial architecture is represented by an early cob house, **Broadgreen House** (1855), whose interior has been restored in period style. Another historic homestead, **Isel House**, is surrounded by century-old trees, rhododendrons and azaleas in the superb setting of Isel Park. Both are in the neighbouring suburb of Stoke, a 10-minute drive from the city centre.

*Visitor information centre, Trafalgar and Halifax streets. Tel: 03 548 2304. Open: daily 7.15am–5pm (closes later in summer).*
*Craft Habitat, Richmond. Tel: 03 544 7481. Just outside town on SH6. Open: weekdays 9am–5pm, weekends 10am–5pm.*
*Suter Art Gallery, Queen's Gardens, Bridge Street. Tel: 03 548 4699. Open: daily 10.30am–4pm. Admission charge.*
*Broadgreen House, Nayland Road, Stoke.*

Motueka is a pleasant base from which to explore the Abel Tasman National Park

The small port of Picton is the gateway to the extensive Marlborough Sounds

Tel: 03 547 7887. Open: daily 2–4.30pm.
Admission charge.
Isel House, Isel Park, The Ridgeway, Stoke.
Open: weekends 2–4pm in summer.
Admission charge.

## NELSON LAKES NATIONAL PARK

The Nelson Lakes National Park covers
102,000 hectares of forests, mountains
and river valleys, and is perhaps best
known for its two beautiful lakes, Rotoiti
and Rotoroa, which nestle beneath scenic
alpine peaks. The main gateway to the
park is the tiny hamlet of St Arnaud, on
the shores of Lake Rotoiti, which is equally
beautiful in summer or in winter when the
ski fields of Rainbow Valley and Mount
Robert beckon. The lake is fringed by
beech forests, and there are opportunities
for boating, fishing, short walks and
picnics. Water taxis ply the lake for short
cruises or drop-offs to hiking tracks.

Lake Rotoroa has fewer facilities (and
more sandflies), but is popular with
fishermen after rainbow trout.
Nelson Lakes Shuttles (tel: 03 521 1887)
operates daily buses.
DOC visitor centre, View Road, St Arnaud.
Tel: 03 521 1806. Open: daily 8am–4.30,

longer during summer. St Arnaud lies 119km
southwest of Nelson on Highway 6 and then
Highway 63.

## PICTON

Lying at the southernmost point of Queen
Charlotte Sound, Picton is the terminus
for the Cook Strait ferry and the starting
point for exploring the Marlborough
Sounds. If you are waiting for a ferry (or a
launch to whisk you off to a secluded
beach) there are a couple of places to visit.

Next to the ferry terminal are the
remnants of the last-surviving convict ship
of the British East India Company, the
Edwin Fox, gradually being restored at the
**Edwin Fox Museum**. Built in 1853, the
teak-hulled ship carried troops to the
Crimean War and convicts to Australia
before ending up as a storage hulk in
Picton's harbour. Also on the waterfront,
the **Picton Museum** is worth a visit for its
whaling relics.
Edwin Fox Museum, Dunbar Wharf. Tel:
03 573 6868. Open: daily 9am–5pm.
Admission charge.
Picton Museum, waterfront. Tel: 03 573
8283. Open: daily 10am–4pm. Admission
charge.

# Kaikoura Peninsula Walkway

Kaikoura is renowned for its marine life (see pages 96–7) and this walkway around the peninsula is a great way of getting close to New Zealand fur seals. The walkway also features ancient Maori stepped *pa* (fortified settlements), limestone caves and wonderful views. This route follows the Clifftop Path (3.7km), returning along the Shoreline Path (4.5km). *Allow 2 hours each way, although the walk is easy and you can complete the circuit much faster if necessary.*

*From Kaikoura, follow the Esplanade south for 5km until you arrive at Point Kean. Park here and take the path marked Clifftop Walk; the well-posted path is easy to follow.*

## 1 CLIFFTOP WALK

A short, steep climb up a zigzag path brings you to the grassy downlands on the clifftop, where the views stretch back inland to

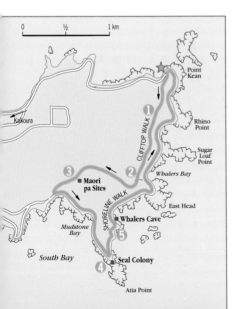

the Kaikoura Mountains and down the coast as far as the Banks Peninsula. The grassy track is a good vantage point from which to observe the gull colonies below: around 10,000 adult red-billed gulls nest here, along with smaller colonies of black-backed gulls and white-fronted terns. You may also spot waders such as turnstones, oystercatchers and herons on the tidal platforms.
*Continue on to Whalers Bay.*

## 2 WHALERS BAY

Whalers Bay once provided safe anchorage for whaling boats, and from the clifftop above the whalers watched and waited, looking for their quarry out to sea. The track used by the whalers to return to their boats descends the cliff face – you can use this as a short cut

Seal pups frolicking amidst sea kelp on the Kaikoura Peninsula coastline

down to the Shoreline Walk if required.
*Follow the signs for South Bay along the clifftop.*

### 3 MAORI *PA* SITES

Taking advantage of the abundant seafood, the Ngati Toa occupied Kaikoura during the 16th century; they were driven south by the Ngai Tahu in the early 19th century, but during the intervening period they occupied at least 14 different *pa* sites on the peninsula. Some of these fortified settlements are clearly visible on this stretch of the track, the characteristic rounded hilltops edged with terracing.
*Descend into South Bay, turning left where the tracks meet to follow the Shoreline Path.*

### 4 SEAL COLONY

Skirting Mudstone Bay you come to Atia Point, which has one of the biggest seal colonies. Around 500 fur seals can be seen here during the winter months, but even in summer dozens of them bask on the rocks: they are so numerous that they often block the path, and you may need to scramble around the rocks to bypass them. Do not provoke the seals (especially large bulls or mothers with pups) as they may bite. Other seal colonies can be seen at East Head and Point Kean.
*Continue around the base of the cliffs.*

### 5 HIDDEN CAVES AND LIMESTONE OUTCROPS

The peninsula is relatively young in geological terms, and the limestone base has been pounded by the sea into many weird and wonderful formations – particularly at Atia Point, which is best appreciated if you look back at it from the succeeding bays. This next section is also riddled with limestone caves, some of which connect one small bay to the next. One of the biggest caves is Whalers Cave, partially obscured by trees at the back of Whalers Bay.
*Cross Whalers Bay and continue past Sugar Loaf Point and Rhino Point to return to the car-park via Point Kean.*

# Central South Island

$S$eparated from one another by the Southern Alps, the west and east coasts of the central part of South Island are as different as chalk and cheese. Hemmed in by the Alps on one side and the Tasman Sea on the other, the west coast is a rugged, wild strip of land where the one constant factor is the almost incessant rain. Driven in by the prevailing westerly winds, this rain falls on the mountain slopes and feeds the lush, dripping rain forests that cloak the landscape. But between the showers you will be rewarded with magnificent views of the Alps' formidable, jagged peaks, tumbling waterfalls and tranquil lakes, and the unusual spectacle of glaciers descending into the rain forests at Fox and Franz Josef.

In the heady gold-rush days of the 1860s, the west coast was one of the busiest, wealthiest areas in the country. Today it is less frenetic, but remnants of those times – such as old machinery, tunnels, water races and ghost towns – lie scattered across the coastal plains. Around Ross and Greymouth

## CENTRAL SOUTH ISLAND

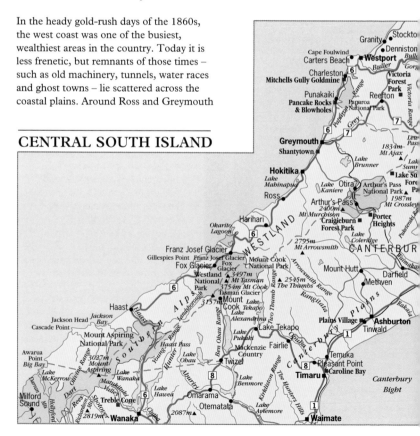

you can still try your hand at gold fossicking or, if you have no luck, you can see how the experts do it at the re-created Shantytown. The west coast is also rich in greenstone (nephrite jade), which was traded by the Maori from the earliest times. The coastal town of Hokitika is well worth a stop to watch the many skilled craftspeople still working this beautiful mineral.

Further south, the Westland coastline reaches an appropriate end in the pristine rain forests and coastal lagoons of the almost untouched World Heritage Area surrounding Haast.

The east coast, by comparison, is intensively cultivated, a patchwork of agricultural lands which seem to stretch forever across the rolling Canterbury Plains. Lying between the plains and the pounding Pacific surf is the city of Christchurch, the second major gateway into New Zealand. To the southeast of this cultured, cosmopolitan city is the Banks Peninsula, a curious outcrop of land formed from the remnants of a sunken volcano, with many bays and beaches to explore and a former French settlement (the most southerly in the world) at Akaroa.

Looping across the Canterbury Plains are a number of shallow, shingle-bed rivers that were almost impossible to navigate until a local engineer invented the jet-boat; these are now as common a feature of outdoor adventure in New Zealand as the helicopter. The Rakaia and Waimakariri rivers are popular for jet-boating, but hikers, cyclists, fishermen, hunters, paragliders and horse-riders will also find plenty to keep them busy around the mountains, lakes and rivers of Canterbury.

Finally, there are the Southern Alps themselves, dominating the scenery on both coasts. Most of the visitor facilities in the Alps are concentrated in the breathtaking Mount Cook National Park and around the shores of the sparkling blue glacial lakes of Pukaki and Tekapo. Here, too, is the mightiest glacier in the southern hemisphere, the Tasman, where ski-planes land on a regular basis. Most people are content simply to absorb the views from atop this 27km giant river of ice, but the more adventurous can ski (weather conditions permitting, and with a guide) down the glacier.

# Christchurch

*C*hristchurch is the South Island's largest city and is also one of the liveliest and most attractive in the country. It has long boasted the epithet of the 'garden city',

## CHRISTCHURCH

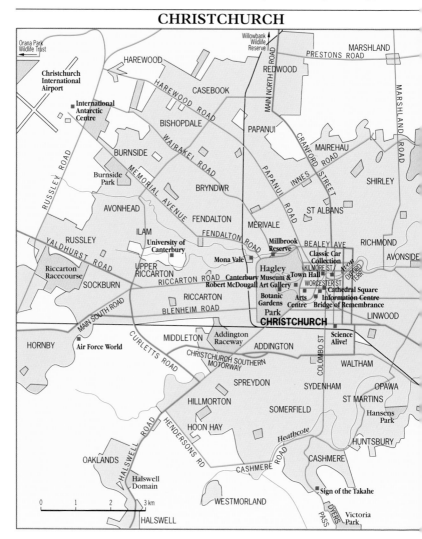

with numerous leafy parks and gardens providing a relaxing backdrop to the well laid out city centre – and with the added bonus of the delightful Avon river meandering between its Gothic stone buildings. Streetside cafés and trendy wine bars have mushroomed in recent years, adding to the vitality of streetlife and complementing a vibrant arts scene with numerous festivals and drama and music performances.

Christchurch is also said to be the most English city in New Zealand. The first four ships carrying the so-called Canterbury Pilgrims arrived at Lyttelton Harbour in 1850, and the newcomers soon established clubs for the very English pastimes of rowing, archery, lawn tennis and cricket. Today, Christchurch has something of a reputation for breeding eccentricity and individualism. Creativity, however, is the flip side of the same coin, and the city has produced enormous numbers of talented craftspeople who you can see at work in the vast Arts Centre complex.

Christchurch is a city made for walking, with many of the top sights within easy reach of Cathedral Square. The historic tram network which follows a route around the central city is another option, and there are also excellent bus services to outlying areas.

Outdoor enthusiasts reckon that, after Queenstown, there is no better place to live in the South Island. In the summer, Pacific Ocean beaches are close by and the Southern Alps are less than an hour's drive away for rock climbing, mountain biking, river rafting and the like. And in winter, there are 12 ski fields from which to choose. Taking advantage of the extensive Canterbury Plains to the west of the city, Christchurch has also become a major centre for hot-air ballooning. Finally, Christchurch is the gateway to the Banks Peninsula (see pages 120–1) and the starting point for the famous TranzAlpine Express rail route across the Southern Alps (see pages 124–5).

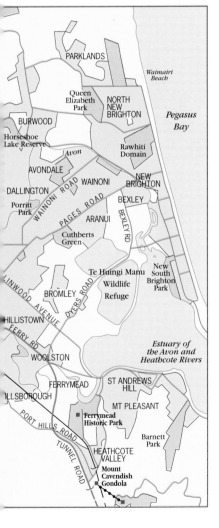

A punt glides along the tranquil River Avon in the heart of Christchurch

## AIR FORCE WORLD

The realistic-looking tableaux that surround many of the 16 classic aircraft in this museum won it a tourism design award in 1991; there are also plenty of hands-on exhibits, video shows and a hall devoted to New Zealand military aviation.

*Wigram RNZAF Base, Main South Road. 20 minutes from downtown. Tel: 03 343 9532. Open: daily 10am–5pm. Admission charge. Bus 8 or 25 or City Circuit Bus.*

## ARTS CENTRE

Housed in a rambling complex of neo-Gothic buildings (once the home of the University of Canterbury), the Arts Centre is a lively mix of galleries, shops, studios and theatres, and cafés, bars and restaurants. You can wander around

peering into small workshops or browsing in half a dozen galleries, then drop in on a lunchtime concert, a dance performance or a foreign-movie screening. The festive weekend market is also well worth visiting, with over a hundred arts and crafts stalls, live entertainment and exotic foods from around the world.

*Worcester Boulevard. Tel: 03 366 0989. Open: weekdays 9.30am–5pm in summer, 10am–4.30pm in winter, weekend market 10am–4pm. Free.*

## AVON RIVER

Winding through the heart of the city, with oaks and willows lining its banks, the Avon adds immeasurably to the enchantment of Christchurch. A good way to get to know the city from this different viewpoint is on a sedate punting trip; alternatively you can hire a canoe or paddle-boat.

*Punt trips depart from behind the information centre. Tel: 03 379 9629 for bookings. Canoes and paddle-boats can be hired at the Antigua Boat Sheds, 2 Cambridge Terrace. Tel: 03 366 5885.*

## BOTANIC GARDENS

The 30-hectare Botanic Gardens, bounded on three sides by the River Avon, are ideal for a relaxing stroll: extensive lawns and bedding displays provide the backdrop to a huge variety of exotic plants. The first trees were planted in 1863 and the collection now encompasses special sections for native plants, heathers, roses, herbs, water plants, primulas and so on, plus a conservatory complex with exotic species.

*Rolleston Avenue. Tel: 03 366 1701. Grounds open: daily 7am until one hour before sunset. Free. Conservatories open: 10.15am–4pm. Tours on a mini-train depart: daily, 11am–4pm from the northern end of the gardens, from where guided tours are also available. Fee payable.*

## CANTERBURY MUSEUM

Housed in one of the city's finest historic buildings, this museum includes displays on Antarctica (Hall of Antarctic Discovery) and New Zealand birds, and also has an award-winning Maori gallery and an Arts of Asia gallery. Future galleries under development include Whalespace (housing a magnificent blue whale skeleton), a second Maori gallery, and a section devoted to colonial arts and costumes.

*Rolleston Avenue. Tel: 03 366 5000. Open: daily 9am–5.30pm/5pm in winter (free). Guided tours (donations): four times daily.*

## CATHEDRAL SQUARE

This spacious, pedestrianised square is a great place to while away a sunny day by enjoying the free show. Almost invariably, atheists and religious fundamentalists mount their step-ladders to battle it out verbally in front of the amused crowds on the cathedral's steps – this is the city's free speech corner, where anything and everything goes. Watch out for the famous Wizard, who is such an adept orator and performer that he has been classified as a 'living work of art' (he usually, but not always, turns up at around 1pm every day). Elsewhere in the square buskers and breakdancers do their stuff, while more contemplative types muse over their next move on a giant outdoor chessboard. There is a regular craft market and a clutch of stalls selling ethnic foods to add to the colour of the city's main focal point.

A giant chess game in Cathedral Square

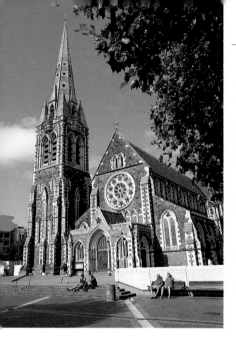

The neo-gothic Cathedral dominates Cathedral Square in Christchurch

## CHRISTCHURCH CATHEDRAL

Built over a period of 40 years and completed in 1904, the cathedral is in neo-gothic style and is worth visiting for the climb (133 steps) to the top of its bell tower, which has good views of the city centre.

*Cathedral Square. Tel: 03 366 0046. Guided tours: weekdays 11am and 2pm, Saturday 11am, Sunday 11.30am. Tower open: daily 8.30am–4pm. Admission charge to tower.*

## FERRYMEAD HISTORIC PARK

The two separate sites of this park (linked by tramway) contain old locomotives and historic vehicles, a replica colonial township, a fire-fighting display and other transport-related exhibits.

*269 Bridle Path Road. Tel: 03 384 1970. Open: daily 10am–4.30pm. Admission charge. Buses 3H or H28 run from downtown.*

## INTERNATIONAL ANTARCTIC CENTRE

Christchurch has been one of the principal gateways to the frozen south since Scott's famous expeditions, and the International Antarctic Centre (next to the airport) is now the main supply and administration base for the New Zealand, American and Italian Antarctic programmes. The award-winning visitor centre within the complex includes a compelling and dramatic audio-visual show, a re-creation of the current Scott Base, the world's only polar aquarium, Snowphone ™, an ice cave and plenty of hands-on exhibits. Highly recommended.

*Orchard Road, Christchurch Airport. 20 minutes by car from downtown. Tel: 03 358 9896. Open: daily 9am–8pm summer, 9am–5.30pm winter. Admission charge.*

## MOUNT CAVENDISH GONDOLA

The gondola scales the city side of Mount Cavendish and terminates at the summit complex, where there are spectacular views over Christchurch and the Banks Peninsula. Within the complex the Time Tunnel recounts the history of the area with some innovative displays, including a volcanic area which blasts out hot air and a superb mock-up (complete with musty smells) of the below-decks scene in an immigrant ship. Shops and fully licensed restaurant.

*Bridle Path Road, Heathcote. Tel: 03 384 0700. Open: daily 10am until late. Admission charge. Regular shuttles depart from the information centre, or take Bus 28 or the City Circuit Bus.*

## ORANA PARK WILDLIFE TRUST

This open-plan zoo covers over 80 hectares and lies to the northwest of the city. There is a drive-through lion enclosure as well as a huge African

plains area covering over 40 hectares; in the Native Fauna and Flora Zone there is a kiwi house, a reptile house and aviaries with rare species such as the Antipodes Island parakeet and the _kaka_.
_McLeans Island Road, Harewood. 20 minutes from downtown. Tel: 03 359 7109. Open: daily from 10am. Admission charge._

## ROBERT MCDOUGALL ART GALLERY

This prestigious gallery (located just behind the museum) has wide-ranging collections of paintings, drawings, prints, sculptures and ceramics, with works by classic and contemporary New Zealand, Australian and European artists.
_Rolleston Avenue, access via the Botanic Gardens. Tel: 03 365 0915. Open: daily 10am–4.30pm (5.30pm in summer). Free._

## SCIENCE ALIVE!

Discovering science and technology through play and hands-on experimentation is the key theme behind this extensive display, aimed at all age groups from pre-teens to adults. Special exhibits often have a local flavour.
_Moorhouse Avenue. 10 minutes walk from the square. Tel: 03 365 5199. Open: daily 9am–5pm. Admission charge. Bus 12 from Cathedral Square._

## WILLOWBANK WILDLIFE RESERVE

This small but well laid out park focuses on indigenous wildlife, although it also has monkeys, camels and other introduced species, and a farmyard section containing rare breeds of colonial animals such as kuni kuni pigs. An unusual feature is the floodlit, night-time viewing, when you can see kiwis and other nocturnal species in their natural bush setting; guided tours are free to dinner guests (see page 171).
_Hussey Road, 20 minutes from downtown. Tel: 03 359 6226. Open: daily 10am–10pm. Admission charge._

A ride in the Mount Cavendish gondola provides spectacular views

# SHEEP

It is an often-quoted fact that there are 20 sheep for every person in New Zealand and, with nearly 57 million sheep compared to 3.5 million people, this figure is not far off the mark.

It was Captain Cook who landed the first sheep in New Zealand, but the two merinos didn't last long and it wasn't until 1834 that the first sizeable flock arrived. The first major 'runs' (as ranches are called here) were in the North Island, but sheep farming developed even more rapidly in the South Island, where there was less forest to clear.

Sheep farming is still an important component in the New Zealand economy

Fortunes had been made from wool exports, but falling prices in the 1880s jeopardised this lucrative commodity. However, refrigerated shipping was invented just in time, and when the *Dunedin* sailed for Britain in 1882

Different breeds of sheep on display in an agricultural show

loaded with sheep carcasses it marked a new era in the country's export trade. With the subsequent increase in meat exports, the merino was gradually replaced by hardy Romneys, great producers of fat lambs. As the wool of the Romney is far coarser than the fine fleece of the merino, production switched to those industries which require stronger, more resilient wools such as the carpet industry.

The biggest farms today are in the South Island, spread over vast areas of comparatively poor land which supports low densities of sheep. These high-country stations often run up to 12,000 or more sheep, so mustering the flocks and bringing them down before the winter snows arrive is a major part of the farming calendar. Previously, this would have been done on horseback, but modern shepherds are more likely to use rugged, all-terrain motorbikes to get around.

Perched on the back of the bike or running alongside will be the shepherd's trusty sheepdogs. Descended from border collie stock, there are two main types: first, there is the 'heading' or 'eye' dog, which prowls silently around the sheep, fixing them with its stare and heading them in the right direction; second, there is the big, noisy 'huntaway', which controls the flocks by barking loudly.

Finally, there are the all-important sheep-shearers, who usually travel together in gangs from station to station. A good shearer can clip up to 300 sheep a day, although the record is an astonishing 831 sheep in nine hours. The average fleece yields around 4.5kg of wool.

# FRANZ JOSEF AND FOX GLACIERS

These two vast glaciers lie at the heart of the Westland National Park, which stretches from the coastline up to some of the highest peaks in New Zealand. The glaciers are unusual in that they extend right down through the forest into the temperate coastal zone, a phenomenon found nowhere else in the world.

The Franz Josef (named after the Austrian emperor by the explorer Julius Haast in 1864) and Fox (named after the country's premier, Sir William Fox, in 1871) are the two largest glaciers of the 140 that lie within the Westland National Park. Close to the bottom of each glacier are the respective villages of Franz Josef and Fox; the constant 'thud-thud' of helicopters taking off from helipads attests to the popularity of aerial sightseeing, with helicopter companies and ski-plane operators offering rides to the top of each glacier. A handful of restaurants, motels and shops provide for everyday needs alongside the helicopter booking offices.

From either village you can drive or walk out to the 'snout' of each glacier. Looming above, the towering blocks of ice (known as *seracs*) lie jumbled together in a dramatic mass which creaks and heaves as blocks split and tumble into the moraine below. Since 1990, the Franz Josef Glacier has been moving at the exceptionally fast rate of around 4m per day.

There are a number of interesting walks in the surrounding forests (details from the DOC centre), as well as twice-daily guided walks on to the glacier itself. Fox Glacier is unusual in that blocks of ice remain buried beneath rock debris downstream of the terminal face, melting to create the milky grey or translucent blue kettle lakes that lie dotted around the bed of the Fox river. One such kettle lake is picturesque Lake Matheson (just south of the village along a short forest track); there are stunning views of the peaks of Mount Cook and Mount Tasman reflected in the waters.

*Guided walks on the glaciers (these should not be attempted on your own) are run by Franz Josef Glacier Guides (tel: 03 752 0763) and Fox Glacier Guides (tel: 03 751 0825).*

*The Westland National Park headquarters*

A helicopter landing is a great way to experience the glaciers

Hopeful visitors pan for gold at Shantytown, outside Greymouth

*in Franz Josef (tel: 03 752 0796) has information leaflets on walks and a display on glaciers. Open: daily 8.30am–7pm, November to April; 9am–5pm May to October. Helicopter 'flightseeing' is available through: Glacier Helicopters (Franz Josef, tel: 03 752 0755; Fox and Franz Josef Heliservices (Franz Josef, tel: 03 7520 793; The Helicopter Line (tel: 03 752 0767); and Westair (tel: 03 7520 716). Mount Cook Airlines (tel: 03 752 0714) operates ski-plane flights.*

*Franz Josef is 172km south of Hokitika, 273km north of Wananka; Fox is 25km further down Highway 6.*

## GREYMOUTH

This former gold and coal centre, today the main commercial centre and largest town on the west coast, is known locally simply as 'Grey'; the tag can seem particularly appropriate on a typically rainy west coast day. **Shantytown**, just outside Greymouth, is a replica 1880s town set in native bushland on the site of a former goldfield. The township features an old bank, a bootshop, printing works, a blacksmiths, a fire station, a 'Chinese den' and a fascinating colonial hospital. Other attractions include a steam-train ride through the bush to an old wooden railway station, gold panning, stage-coach rides and a working replica sawmill.

*Shantytown, Paroa, 11km from Greymouth, signposted off Highway 6. Tel: 03 762 6634. Open: daily from 8.30am. Admission charge.*

*105km south of Westport on Highway 6, 256km from Christchurch.*

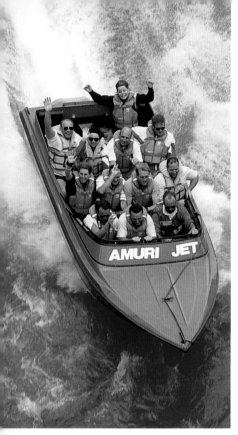

Jet-boating is just one of many adventure activities around Hanmer Springs

## HAAST

Lying as it does at the southernmost end of the Westland coastline, Haast is usually thought of as little more than a staging post for the Haast Pass across the Southern Alps into Otago. This is about to change, however, as the Haast area achieves greater recognition for the magnificent rain forests, coastal lagoons and wetlands (the most extensive in the country) that surround it. The region was designated the South West New Zealand World Heritage Area by Unesco in 1991, and the excellent World Heritage Visitor Centre opened on the banks of the Haast river in 1993. The centre has a series of first-rate displays on early Maori settlers, the abundant local wildlife, swamp forests and the unique sand-dune forests near by. Staff can also provide information on local walks, jet-boating on the Haast river, fishing (the coastal lagoons are renowned for their whitebait), hiking and helicopter rides.

*120km southwest of Fox Glacier, 345km southwest of Greymouth. Visitor Centre, PO Box 50, Haast. Tel: 03 750 0809. Open: daily 8.30am–4pm.*

## HANMER SPRINGS

First discovered by Maori hunters, who gave them the name Waitapu ('Sacred Waters'), these thermal springs were rediscovered by a local farmer in 1859 and, by the turn of the century, were the focus of a popular sanitorium. Today the springs are incorporated into a modern, open-air resort complex, the **Hanmer Springs Thermal Reserve**, located in the centre of this tranquil little alpine village. If you want some action and adventure before soaking away your aches and pains in the pools, the area offers an enormous number of activities, from golf to rafting, jet-boating, fishing, bungee-jumping, climbing and horse-trekking. There are plenty of walks in the nearby Hanmer Forest Park and further afield; details of these and all outdoor activities are available from the information centre.

*Thermal Reserve, PO Box 30, Hanmer Springs. Tel: 03 315 7511. Open: daily 10am–9pm. Admission charge.*
*Hurunui Visitor Information Centre, Hanmer Springs. Tel: 03 315 7128. Open: daily 10am–6pm in summer, 10am–4.30pm in winter.*

*136km north of Christchurch.*

## HOKITIKA

The next major town south of Greymouth is Hokitika, first settled by Maori in search of greenstone and later by Europeans in the gold rush of the 1860s. The town boomed briefly before the prospectors moved on elsewhere. Today, life centres around farming, fishing and tourism, although some gold-mining is still carried out.

Hokitika is an attractive town which has become a focus for local craftspeople and is also well known as a centre for greenstone carving. There are several workshops in town where you can watch these massive blocks being shaped and fashioned into intricate designs for pendants, sculptures and so on; this is a fascinating process, and it costs nothing to wander around watching the greenstone carvers at work. There are numerous other outlets in town for arts and crafts such as pottery, textiles, wood carvings, and hand-crafted jewellery made from gold nuggets found in the area. The history of the area is narrated in the **West Coast Historical Museum**, where there is a well-constructed audio-visual show covering both greenstone and gold discoveries in the region amongst the other displays.

Just south of town is the **Phelp's Gold Mine**, which has displays on old-time gold-mining as well as offering the chance to see how it is done today in a large-scale mining operation. There are also bush walks through old mine workings and tunnels.

*West Coast Historical Museum, Tancred Street. Tel: 03 755 6898. Open: daily 9.30am–5pm. Admission charge.*

*Most of the Tancred Street shops are open seven days a week.*

*Phelp's Gold Mine, 2km south of town on Highway 6. Tel: 03 755 7766. Open: daily 9am–5pm. Admission charge.*

*46km south of Greymouth on Highway 6.*

Open-air thermal pools at Hanmer Springs

The south face of Mount Cook, which at 3,763m is the highest peak in New Zealand

## MOUNT COOK NATIONAL PARK

Covering just over 70,000 hectares, the Mount Cook National Park runs in a narrow strip down the eastern side of the Southern Alps. Within this relatively small area are found 22 of the 27 highest peaks in New Zealand, including, of course, the most well-known of them all, Mount Cook itself. This is an area of great natural beauty, where alpine scrub and forests are interspersed with glacial lakes that reflect the snow-capped crests soaring above. The park also includes the impressive 28km-long Tasman Glacier, the largest glacier in the southern hemisphere outside of Antarctica.

Known as Aoraki by the Maori, Mount Cook was renamed by Captain Stokes who sighted it from his survey ship in 1851. The first attempt to climb the peak was made in 1882 by Rev Green, an Irishman, but storms prevented him reaching the summit and it wasn't until 1894 that it was eventually conquered by three New Zealanders (Fyfe, Graham and Clarke). Sir Edmund Hillary trained here before becoming the first man to climb Mount Everest in 1953, and it remains one of the finest mountaineering regions in the world, with well-equipped high-level mountain huts for climbers' use. Walkers are restricted to the valley floor, but there are still some superb short walks near the base (see pages 122–3).

The central focus of the national park is Mount Cook village, where there is a youth hostel, campsite, self-contained chalets and the famous Hermitage Hotel. The visitor centre can provide details on hut fees, routes and weather conditions for climbers.

More than 300 species of plants are found within the park, including the famed Mount Cook lily (*Ranunculus lyallii*), the largest buttercup in the world. Of the 40 species of birds, the most noticeable is the kea, well known for pilfering hikers' belongings. Hunting of the Himalayan thar and European chamois (both of which destroy vegetation) is encouraged.

Skiing is possible from July to October, but the only way up to the available slopes is by ski-plane or helicopter. The most spectacular run is the descent of the Tasman Glacier, suitable only for experienced and advanced snowboarders or skiers. Aerial sightseeing is another popular option and provides opportunities for some breathtaking photographs of the peaks and glaciers. Mount Cook Airlines offers a number of options with snow landings, as well as a 'grand circle' tour which crosses the Alps over to the Franz Josef and Fox glaciers. Helicopter flights are also available.

*Visitor centre, PO Box 5, Mount Cook. Tel: 03 435 1895. Open: daily 8am–5pm (7pm in summer).*
*Mount Cook Airlines, Mount Cook Airport. Tel: 03 435 1849; Note: petrol can only be obtained in Mount Cook by credit card with a PIN number suitable for use in New Zealand.*

*333km west of Christchurch.*

## PAPAROA NATIONAL PARK

The coastal road between Westport and Greymouth is at its most spectacular as it passes the fringes of the Paparoa National Park, located about half-way between the two towns. Created in 1987, the national park covers around 30,000 hectares.

On the coastal strip, steep limestone cliffs plunge down to the sea, creating a subtropical microclimate where tree ferns and nikau palms thrive. Inland, the park is a virtually untouched wilderness with unusual limestone karst formations, large caves and waterfalls. The undisturbed nature of Paparoa means that it is a good area for bird-watching (tuis, fantails, grey warblers, New Zealand pigeons and bellbirds are commonly spotted). At the heart of the park is the Paparoa Range, a rugged series of peaks and pinnacles covered in virtually impenetrable bush and often shrouded in clouds. The best-known walking route through the park is the Inland Pack Track, but there are also several short walks which start from Punakaiki. For details on the local DOC visitor centre and how to reach the park, see Punakaiki (page 118).

The *kereru* (native pigeon), found in the Paparoa National Park

## PUNAKAIKI

Punakaiki is best known for its extraordinary Pancake Rocks, reached by a short, 15-minute walk from the main road, suitable for wheelchairs. The stratified coastal limestone here has been weathered into a dramatic formation that looks just like a stack of giant pancakes; in rough conditions the sea forces itself up through fissures in the 'pancakes' to form spectacular blowholes.

The DOC visitor centre at Punakaiki can provide details on short walks in the area which lead back into the rain forests of the Paparoa National Park (see page 117).

*The DOC visitor centre is on the main road. Tel: 03 731 1895. Open: daily 8am–4.30pm (closes later in summer).*

*57km south of Westport, 47km north of Greymouth on Highway 6.*

## ROSS

Early prospectors descended on Ross in their thousands at the turn of the century to fossick in the creeks running down from Mount Greenland. The Ross Historic Goldfields lie just off the highway through town; the information centre is located in an old Bank of New South Wales building (1870) at the entrance. Just across from the information centre is the Miner's Cottage, dating back to 1885. The Jones Flat Walkway leads from the information centre up to the old workings, which include miles of intertwined water races and dams that were used to bring water to the sluicing claims.

*Information centre (tel: 03 755 4077). Open: daily 9am–4pm (later in summer).*

*30km southwest of Hokitika.*

A memorial to hard-working sheep dogs, on the shores of Lake Tekapo

## TEKAPO

This small settlement straddles the road leading from Mount Cook National Park back down to the coast, and where 20km-long Lake Tekapo empties into the Tekapo river with the first of the hydroelectric stations linked to the Waitaki River system. Surrounded by tussock-clad hills, the milky turquoise lake is noted for its trout fishing. On the edge of Tekapo is the famous Church of the Good Shepherd, a sublime stone-clad chapel erected as a memorial to pioneer farmers in the area.
*105km west of Timaru.*

## TIMARU

This large coastal port city, lying roughly midway between Christchurch and Dunedin, is famous for its annual carnival, which takes place on sandy Caroline Bay for three weeks at Christmas.
*164km south of Christchurch, 202km north of Dunedin.*

## TWIZEL

This town, established as the centre for the upper Waitaki Valley hydroelectric development, lies just half an hour's drive from Mount Cook village, making it a convenient base for exploring the national park and the surrounding Waitaki River and Mackenzie basin. The road from Twizel to Mount Cook runs alongside lovely Lake Pukaki, one of the four Mackenzie Basin lakes.

Just outside town is the Black Stilt Aviary, a DOC centre for a breeding programme aimed at saving this endangered species. Once common throughout New Zealand, the black stilt's habitat is now confined to the Mackenzie Basin. Guided tours include close-up views of captive stilts and explanations of the breeding programme and rearing aviaries.
*Black Stilt Aviary, 3km south of town on SH8. Open: daily from 10am in summer (closed weekends in winter). Admission charge. It is essential that tours are booked in advance at the DOC visitor centre, Wairepo Road, Twizel. Tel: 03 435 0801.*

*162km west of Timaru.*

## WESTPORT

Gold-mining and, later, coal-mining formed the basis of Westport's prosperity. If you are passing through there are some good exhibits on coal-mining in the aptly named Coaltown museum.

Nearby Cape Foulwind is one of six breeding colonies on the west coast for the New Zealand fur seal. Walkways lead to a series of wooden platforms on the clifftops, from where you can observe the seals below.
*Coaltown, Queen Street South, signposted from the town centre. Tel: 03 789 8204. Open: daily 8.30am–5.30pm (9am–4.30 in winter). Admission charge.*
*Cape Foulwind is 12km west of town on Highway 65A.*

The Pancake Rocks at Punakaiki are one of the most striking features of Paparoa National Park

*105km north of Greymouth.*

# Banks Peninsula

The Banks Peninsula is the site of the only attempt at a settlement by the French in New Zealand, and its offshore waters are home to one of the highest concentrations of the world's smallest and rarest marine dolphins, the Hector's dolphin. *Allow a full day for this 185km round trip from Christchurch.*

*Leave Christchurch on the SH75, following signs for Akaroa. Turning away from the sea past Little River, the road climbs up and over the crater rim and descends into Barry's Bay.*

### 1 BARRY'S BAY

Banks Peninsula was one of the first areas in New Zealand to produce cheese (commercial shipments were sent to Australia as early as the 1850s). This tradition continues today at the cheese factory in Barry's Bay, where you can

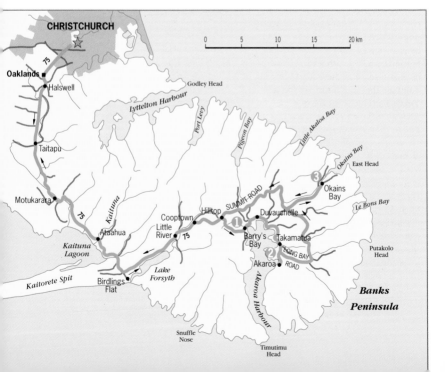

watch cheese being made through the gallery window.
*Continue around the bay to Akaroa.*

## 2 AKAROA

In 1838, Jean Langlois, captain of a whaling ship, negotiated to buy Banks Peninsula from the local Maori. He assembled a group of 63 colonists on his return to France, but by the time they arrived back in New Zealand the Maori had already ceded sovereignty to the British. The settlers still chose to remain, founding Akaroa. Today, this is a delightful township, with considerable emphasis placed on the French connection in the shops, bars and restaurants.

One French colonist's home, the Langlois-Eteveneaux Cottage, now houses the small Akaroa Museum, with exhibits on Maori life on the peninsula, and whaling. Further along the seafront, two plaques mark the landing site of the original settlers on 16 August, 1840. Near by is a jetty from which you can take harbour cruises, with a reasonable chance of seeing some of the 600 to 700 Hector's dolphins that inhabit the harbour.
*Turning back towards Barry's Bay, take Long Bay Road and follow the signs for Okains Bay, 19km from Akaroa.*

## 3 OKAINS BAY

This lovely bay is a popular picnic spot, with the beach and lagoon providing safe, sheltered swimming. In such a remote location it comes as a surprise to find a fascinating collection of artefacts in the Maori and Colonial Museum, located at the entrance to the village. This started as a private collection and has since grown to include a working blacksmith's shop, horse-drawn carriages and an old 'slab cottage', built from large, adzed slabs of totara wood. The Maori collection is

extraordinary and many rare objects are on display, including war weapons, flax cloaks, adzes, and an unusual and valuable 'god stick' dating back to AD 1400. There is also a war canoe (1867), and one of the only fully carved meeting-houses in the South Island.
*Return to Christchurch along the panoramic Summit Road, rejoining the SH75 at the Hilltop junction.*

Rural surroundings of the Banks Peninsula

---

**Barry's Bay Cheese Factory**
Akaroa (tel: 03 304 5809). Open: weekdays 8am–5pm, weekends 9.30am–5pm, viewing only on alternate days between October and April.
Akaroa can also be reached on the Akaroa Shuttle (tel: 03 379 9629). Twice-daily departures in each direction.
**Akaroa Museum**
rue Lavaud and rue Balguerie (tel: 03 304 7614). Open: daily 10.30am–4.30pm. Admission charge.
**Maori and Colonial Museum**
Okains Bay (tel: 03 304 8611). Open: daily 10am–5pm. Admission charge.

# Hooker Valley

The Hooker Valley Walk is one of the best walks in the Mount Cook National Park, with wonderful panoramas of the surrounding ranges and of Mount Cook itself. It runs along a gentle gradient, crossing the Hooker river twice on swingbridges and meandering through alpine pasturelands, before finishing at the lovely terminal lake below the Hooker Glacier. Most people return from here (a three- or four-hour round trip), but if you haven't yet had your fill of views you can continue up to the Hooker Hut (allow another two hours).

*From the Hermitage, follow the Kea Point Track across the Hooker Flats, crossing the road and then joining the Hooker Valley Track.*

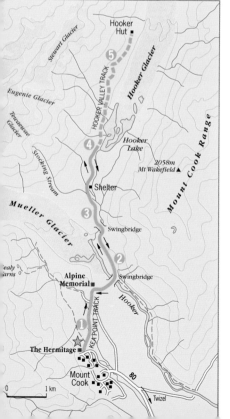

## 1 CAMPSITE TO HOOKER RIVER

The path zigzags between tussock mounds past the site of the original Hermitage (1884–1913) before reaching the Alpine Memorial, which you can climb up to for good views of the Hooker Valley ahead. From the memorial, the track loops up and around low, hummocky hills of moraine (glacial debris), before arriving alongside the Hooker river.
*Cross the first swingbridge.*

## 2 HOOKER VALLEY

Leading away to the left is the grey, debris-ridden expanse of the Mueller Glacier, with the mighty hanging glaciers and icefalls of Mount Sefton towering above it. The other peaks in the Main Divide of the Southern Alps curve round on the north side of the Hooker Valley, with Mount Cook now visible at the head of the valley. The track continues beneath a series of small bluffs at the foot of Mount Wakefield before arriving at the second swingbridge.

The terminal lake of the Hooker Glacier, with Mount Cook rising up in the background

*Cross the Hooker river again on the second swingbridge.*

### 3 ALPINE PASTURES

The great ice faces of Mount Cook's southern flank dominate the view as the track leaves the Hooker river and crosses alpine pastureland to reach an open shelter at Stocking Stream, where there is an orientation table. Grasses and alpine plants cover the flatlands, with dense bushes clinging to the older moraine ridges above. In spring and summer these alpine meadows are a glorious profusion of buttercups (including the famous Mount Cook lily), giving way to daisies and, in the autumn, gentians.

*Continue on past the Stocking Stream shelter.*

### 4 HOOKER LAKE AND GLACIER

A gentle climb alongside the river brings you to the terminal lake (Hooker Lake) at the foot of the Hooker Glacier. Ice floes on the lake's aquamarine waters create a photogenic foreground to the towering bulk of Mount Cook to the west.

*Return the way you came or, if time allows, continue up to the Hooker Hut.*

### 5 HOOKER LAKE TO HOOKER HUT

The route follows the edge of the lake and then branches off diagonally upwards across the terminal moraine, where it is marked by a series of cairns. The track crosses two side-streams on top of the moraine wall before zigzagging down to the hut in its sheltered basin. From here there are terrific views of Mount Cook, with the Noeline and Mona glaciers spilling down into the Hooker. The Hooker Hut is the starting point for the Copland Pass which crosses the Alps, but you should not proceed beyond here unless properly equipped.

# TranzAlpine Express

This 233km journey from Christchurch to Greymouth is one of the classics of rail travel, connecting the two coastlines via the mountain passes of the Southern Alps on a narrow-gauge, single-track line which winds its way through tunnels and along impressive viaducts spanning deep canyons.

## 1 THE CANTERBURY PLAINS

Leaving Christchurch station behind, the train crosses the rolling Canterbury Plains and passes through several small towns before halting at Springfield, the last stop before the climb into the mountains. The Southern Alps, dominated here by Mount Hutt (2,188m), loom ahead.

## 2 SPRINGFIELD TO ARTHUR'S PASS

This is undoubtedly one of the most spectacular sections of the journey – try to get a seat on the right-hand side of the observation car if possible. The train soon crosses Big Kowai Viaduct, the first of five high viaducts that span rushing mountain torrents, and then enters the first of 16 tunnels chiselled through the rock. As you emerge from the sixth tunnel you will see the Waimakariri river way below, a raging blue-green snake twisting through the canyon. Next is Staircase Viaduct, the highest and most impressive on the line – at a height of 73m it could easily accommodate Christchurch Cathedral with room to spare. All the tunnels on this route are relatively short (the longest, Tunnel 10, is just 600m long), although in the days of steam trains even these were long enough to nearly suffocate the footplate crews. *Once past Broken River Viaduct (with spectacular views back down the Waimakariri river), the train clings to the northwest side of Broken River Gorge. Six tunnels are then passed in quick succession, before Sloven's Creek Viaduct is crossed and the broad, open valleys of the uplands are entered.*

## 3 ARTHUR'S PASS

This small township is the starting point for hikes into the surrounding Arthur's Pass National Park, and at 737m above sea-level it is the highest railway station in New Zealand. Arthur's Pass was once the change-over point from steam to electric locomotives, as the next section is the steepest on the route.

## 4 ARTHUR'S PASS TO OTIRA

After a brief halt at Arthur's Pass, the TranzAlpine enters the 8.5km-long Otira Tunnel for the 400m descent to Otira; when it first opened in 1918 the tunnel was the longest in the British Empire, and seventh longest in the world. The TranzAlpine cruises through in both directions with its diesel-electric locomotive, but when the coal trains make the long haul up from Greymouth to Arthur's Pass it takes up to four electric locomotives to overcome the gradient.

The TranzAlpine departs Christchurch at 9am daily, arriving in Greymouth at 1.30pm. The train stops at Arthur's Pass briefly then continues on through the Otira Tunnel. There is a full on-board buffet and bar service. Bookings can be made with any NZ Rail accredited travel agent or through NZ Rail's central reservations (tel: 0800 802 802 toll-free).

The road over Arthur's Pass, also a spectacular train ride

## 5 OTIRA TO GREYMOUTH

On the left after leaving Otira station you will see the escape track for runaway trains coming down from Arthur's Pass; this has been used at least twice, in 1957 and 1962, with locomotives failing to hold on the 1-in-33 grade track.

From here on the contrast with the east coast landscapes is immediately apparent, the rain forests of Westland spreading out across the hillsides. Skirting the edges of Lake Poerua and Lake Brunner, the TranzAlpine meets up with the west coast railway and follows the Grey river into Greymouth itself.

# THE DEEP SOUTH

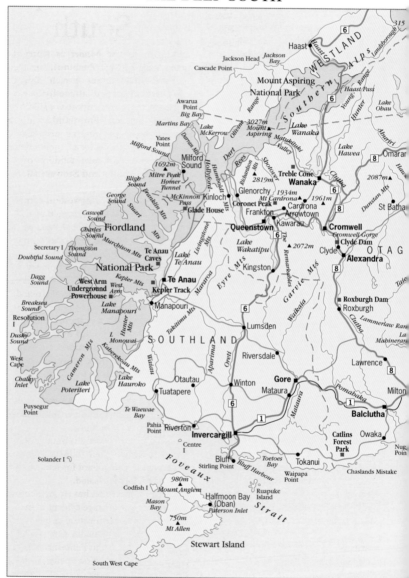

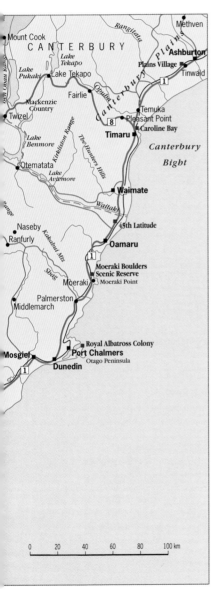

# The Deep South

*K*nown to the Maori as Muruhiku (the 'tail' of New Zealand), the Deep South encompasses a rich diversity of landscapes and attractions, ranging from the splendours of Milford Sound in the Fiordland National Park to the impressive architecture of Dunedin, historic gold-mining towns and the rare wildlife of the Otago Peninsula and Stewart Island.

Almost the entire southwestern corner of the South Island is occupied by the massive Fiordland National Park, whose glaciated landscapes, inland lakes and deep fiords provide some of the most spell-binding scenery in the country.

The lakeside resort of Te Anau is one of the main access points to Fiordland, as is the busy resort of Queenstown on the shore of Lake Wakatipu. Outdoor adventures (from guided hiking to tranquil lake or fiord cruises) are well catered for, with Queenstown providing more thrills and spills than almost any other location in New Zealand – rafting, bungee-jumping, skydiving, and much else besides is on offer to anyone willing to take up the challenge.

Adjoining Fiordland is Southland, with the regional capital, Invercargill, serving as a springboard for remote and unspoiled Stewart Island.

The Otago region has strong Scottish connections, a heritage evident in the well-preserved architecture of the regional capital, Dunedin. On the city's doorstep is the Otago Peninsula, where royal albatrosses and rare penguins can be seen at remarkably close quarters.

## ALEXANDRA

Built on the back of the Otago gold rushes, Alexandra later turned to fruit farming and is a thriving service centre for the surrounding agricultural community. Tourism is now also taking off, with adventure activities which include jetboating and kayaking in the nearby Roxburgh Gorge and mountain biking and 4WD tours in the rugged terrain which surrounds the town. Local wineries and the country's first freshwater crayfish farm can also be visited.

*93km southeast of Queenstown.*

The Great Hall in Olveston, a historic mansion in Dunedin

## ARROWTOWN

This picturesque gold-mining town is nearly always full of people taking snap-shots of its old stone-miner's cottages and, in the autumn, of the glorious foliage on the trees lining Buckingham Street and the banks of the Arrow river. Ironically, it was the complete lack of trees in the area that forced the gold-miners of the 1860s to build in stone, and this also led later arrivals to plant the non-indigenous broadleaved trees – such as sycamore and oak – which give Arrowtown its unique appeal today.

The story of those early pioneering days is recounted in the **Lakes District Museum**, where you can also pick up the leaflet 'Historic Arrowtown' which will guide you around over 40 historic buildings in the township (although many are private houses, and can only be viewed from the street).

*Lakes District Museum, Buckingham Street. Tel: 03 442 1824. Open: daily 9am–5pm. Admission charge.*

*20km northeast of Queenstown, with regular tours on the Double Decker Red Bus (tel: 03 442 6067).*

## DUNEDIN

Sprawling in a horseshoe shape around the head of the deep-water inlet of Otago Harbour, Dunedin is an attractive, solidly built city that was originally founded by Scottish settlers. It grew prosperous on the back of the 1860s gold rush in Central Otago and was the wealthiest city in New Zealand at the turn of the century. The legacy of those days is visible in the numerous well-preserved Victorian and Edwardian buildings that lie dotted about the city, such as the University of Otago (1869), the Railway Station (1906), the

Municipal Chambers (1880) and the Otago Boys' High School (1885).

Dunedin retains a distinctive Scottish heritage; it has the country's only whisky distillery, Scottish Week is celebrated with bagpipe-playing and highland flings in March, and you can even arrange a haggis ceremony or buy a kilt here. The South Island's second-largest city is also a thriving university town and cultural centre, with numerous exhibitions, concerts and arts festivals. Additionally, the city makes a convenient base for visiting the wonderful Otago Peninsula (see page 133), right on the doorstep.

### The Octagon

Dominated by a statue of the Scottish bard Robbie Burns, the Octagon is the focal centre of the city and has a clutch of lively cafés and restaurants along its eastern side. On the western side you will find the visitor centre (housed in the old Municipal Chambers) and the Anglican St Paul's Cathedral, built from Oamaru stone in 1919.

### Olveston

Built at the turn of the century, Olveston is a gracious Jacobean stone mansion with a wealth of decorative detail (such as mullioned windows and bronze chandeliers), and a well-preserved collection of furnishings, treasured artefacts and paintings collected by the Theomin family who lived here. The mansion's 35 rooms are a testament to the family's Edwardian lifestyle.

*42 Royal Terrace. Tel: 03 477 3320. Open: daily, with one-hour guided tours six times daily 9.30am–4pm. Admission charge.*

### Otago Settlers Museum

Billed as 'New Zealand's leading collection of colonial memorabilia', this

A multicoloured portal outside the Otago Settlers Museum, Dunedin

museum, a short distance west of the station, houses many fascinating relics alongside priceless archives, manuscripts and photographs.

*220 Cumberland Street. Tel: 03 477 5052. Open: weekdays 10am–5pm, weekends 1–5pm. Admission charge.*

### Otago Museum

Founded in 1868 and renowned for its Maori and Pacific Island artefacts (particularly carved greenstone and other items from the southern Maori), the museum also has a good natural history section with life-size displays of moas, a maritime hall and a collection of decorative arts from Asia. The numerous hands-on science exhibits in the exciting Discovery World section should keep the kids happy.

*419 Great King Street. Tel: 03 477 2372. Open: weekdays 10am–5pm, weekends 1–5pm. Museum free; admission charge to Discovery World.*

A beautiful alpine stream flowing through the Fiordland National Park

## FIORDLAND NATIONAL PARK

Spread across 12,000sq km in the most remote corner of the South Island is Fiordland, the largest national park in New Zealand and one of the largest in the world. The park's serrated coastline is punctuated by beautiful fiords which reach back into the bush-clad hills and mountains. In the hinterland, deep, branching lakes – also carved out by glaciers – add further allure to this stunning region. The impenetrability of Fiordland's rain forests and rugged mountains have kept intruders at bay for centuries, and much of the region remains an unspoiled wilderness where rare species – such as the blue duck and

the kakapo – have managed to retain a foothold. The high annual rainfall creates hundreds of cascading waterfalls and often leads to dramatic landslips as it washes away whole hillsides of vegetation.

The most northerly of the 14 fiords along the coast is Milford Sound, dominated by the majestic Mitre Peak. The hanging valleys that flank the fiord drain Milford's phenomenal annual rainfall (at 6,400mm, the country's highest) into a series of spectacular waterfalls, while the fiord's sheer walls (rising 1,200m vertically from the sea) dwarf even the biggest visiting cruise liners as they make their way down the sound. Milford is the most accessible and heavily visited of the fiords. You can reach it by coach tour, drive there from Te Anau (see pages 140–1), or fly in by helicopter or light aeroplane; another option is to walk in along the famous Milford Track.

The main gateway to Fiordland is the lakeside township of **Te Anau**, which has a wide range of accommodation and activities on offer. The 53km-long Lake Te Anau is the largest in the South Island, and cruises across to the Te Anau Caves are popular; accessible only by boat, these feature underground waterfalls and a glow-worm grotto.

To the south of Te Anau lies beautiful **Lake Manapouri**, once threatened by a hydroelectric scheme. The huge public outcry that greeted this plan led to the idea being vetoed, and although a power plant was still built, it was sited underground to placate the protestors. Tours of the giant West Arm Underground Powerhouse (200m underground and reached via a 2km-long spiral access tunnel) can be combined with a trip onwards over the mountains across the Wilmot Pass to Doubtful

Sound. This lovely fiord is home to fur seals, dusky and bottlenose dolphins, and the Fiordland crested penguin.

*The main agency for tours and activities is Fiordland Travel, Lake Front, Te Anau. Tel: 03 249 7416. Tours to the Te Anau Caves depart: daily 2pm and 8.15pm. Lake Manapouri and power station tours depart: twice daily, with the morning departure only continuing on to Doubtful Sound.*

*Te Anau lies 167km from Queenstown.*

### INVERCARGILL

This is the southernmost city in New Zealand and is the main gateway to Stewart Island (see page 136). If you are passing through, the **Southland Museum and Art Gallery** (housed inside a giant pyramid) is a must; the

exhibits span hundreds of years of cultural and natural history including New Zealand's subantarctic islands, with some stunning photography and good audio-visual effects.

Invercargill is also the starting point (or the finish, depending on which way you're travelling) of the excellent Southern Scenic Route, which traverses the remote southeastern coastline up to Balclutha. This 172km route encompasses the untouched coastal forests of the Catlins (home to many rare birds) as well as the fossilised remains of 180-million-year-old trees at Curio Bay and colonies of seals, yellow-eyed penguins, gannets and sooty sheerwaters.

*Southlands Museum and Art Gallery, Queens Park. Tel: 03 218 9753. Open: weekdays 9am–5pm, weekends 10am–5pm. Admission charge.*

*225km southwest of Dunedin.*

Rugged peaks and deep glacial valleys are characteristic features of Fiordland

The Moeraki Boulders look like giant marbles on the seashore

## MOERAKI

Just outside this small fishing port is the Moeraki Boulders Scenic Reserve, a small area of beach on which several spherical boulders lie. These geological curiosities were formed in the surrounding mudstone some 60 million years ago when North Otago was covered by the ocean; there are around 50 along this section of coast, the largest of which measure over 2m in diameter. There is a boardwalk running around the low cliffs and along the beach.

*38km south of Oamaru, 78km north of Dunedin. The Reserve is signposted off the main road (SH1), with open access.*

## OAMARU

Oamaru is the main coastal town in North Otago and is best known for its exceptionally pure creamy white limestone, used to good effect in many fine public buildings in the last century. On tree-lined Thames Street, these buildings include the National Bank, the Bank of New South Wales (now an art gallery) and the first Post Office (now a restaurant). The Old Harbour area is gradually being restored as a typical Victorian waterfront village, with some of the huge old warehouses, grain and wool stores being converted into premises for craftworkers among others. Oamaru is noted for its extensive **Public Gardens**; established in 1876, these include a wallaby park, fountains, statues and floral displays.

Just outside Oamaru is a blue penguin colony where you can see these rare animals returning to their nesting sites each night from two viewing platforms. There is also a yellow-eyed penguin colony on Bushy Beach.

*One-hour tours of the Old Harbour area can be booked through the Historic Oamaru Project Centre in the old Criterion Hotel, Tyne Street. Tel: 03 434 5385. Open: weekdays 9am–5pm, weekends and holidays 10am–5pm.*

*Oamaru Public Gardens, Severn Street. Details on viewing times and access regulations to both penguin colonies are available from Oamaru Blue Penguin Colony, Oamaru. Tel: 03 434 1718.*

*250km south of Christchurch, 116km north of Dunedin.*

Blue penguins nest near Oamaru

## OTAGO PENINSULA

Jutting out from Dunedin and protecting its harbour from the Pacific Ocean is the Otago Peninsula, remarkable for the variety of wildlife that is concentrated here so close to a city centre. New Zealand fur seals are numerous around the coastline, and colonies of yellow-eyed and blue penguins nest on several beaches. The peninsula's scenic inlets are also home to large numbers of wading and water fowl, and, to cap it all, Taiaroa Head boasts the only albatross nesting site in the world which exists this close to civilisation.

The peninsula also has its man-made attractions, prime amongst which is **Larnach Castle** in its spectacular setting overlooking the sea and the peninsula. The castle is the legacy of William Larnach, whose family had a colourful history (Larnach himself committed suicide in 1898 due to a series of financial disasters). Built between 1871 and 1887, the castle has a huge ballroom, a skilful Georgian hanging staircase, and several fine Italian marble fireplaces and elaborately decorated ceilings. The castle is surrounded by 14 hectares of attractive gardens.

Another popular spot is the **Glenfalloch Gardens** on the seashore, with 12 hectares of rhododendrons, azaleas, magnolias, fuchsias and roses. Further along the coast road, the New Zealand Marine Studies Centre and Trustbank Aquarium (the largest marine research centre in the country) has a public **aquarium** in its basement which houses some of the unusual and fascinating species that can be found around the rocky coastlines of the peninsula, and a touch tank where you can handle invertebrates and other animals.

For more details on wildlife and other attractions in the area, see pages 138–9.
*Larnach Castle, PO Box 1350, Camp Road, Dunedin. 15km from central Dunedin, off Castlewood Road. 9km from central Dunedin on the Portobello Road. Tel: 03 476 1616. Open: daily 9am–5pm. Admission charge.*
*Glenfalloch Gardens, PO Box 492, Dunedin. Tel: 03 476 1006. Open: daily dawn to dusk. Entry by donation.*
*New Zealand Marine Studies Centre, PO Box 8, Dunedin. Tel: 03 478 0011. Open: daily noon–4pm in summer, weekends and public holidays noon–4.30pm in winter. Admission charge.*

A church in Oamaru, noted for its pure Oamaru stone

# Queenstown

*T*he wonderful natural setting of Queenstown on the shores of Lake Wakatipu, with the dramatic Remarkables mountain range rising up behind it, would be enviable even if the town had no other assets – and it does by the bucketload. The town is New Zealand's premier tourist resort and has a remarkable range of activities from which to choose: sensational helicopter adventures, tandem parachute or parapente jumps, white-water surfing, flightseeing in an old DC3 and jet-boating – not to mention A J Hackett's famous bungee-jumping enterprise (see page 147).

The ultimate Queenstown thrill is the 'Awesome Foursome', an adrenalin-pumping day that combines a helicopter ride with jet-boating, white-water rafting and a bungee jump. Less hair-raising activities include sedate lake cruises, back-country tours, or horse-trekking; in winter, the nearby Coronet Peak and Remarkables ski fields (rated among the best in the country) come into their own.

Efficient, computerised booking offices line Queenstown's main street, with only a credit-card voucher standing between you and the adventure of a lifetime. And when you have had enough serious fun, relax in one of the town's 100 or so restaurants, bars and eateries, many of which have live music. The resort also has an excellent range of shops, most staying open until 9pm, seven days a week. Over 40 hotels and

Queenstown, one of the country's busiest resorts, lies on the shores of Lake Wakatipu

motels and 26 guest-houses and hostels cater to the needs of the annual influx of over half a million visitors.

As you might expect, Queenstown buzzes both day and night, a cosmopolitan enclave surrounded by the seductive wilderness of central Otago. For details on individual adventure activities, see pages 146–50.

The TSS *Earnslaw* is a vintage steamer which still plies the lake waters daily

### KIWI AND BIRDLIFE PARK
The park has a nocturnal kiwi house, as well as aviaries, ponds and landscaped gardens where other native birds can be seen.
*Bevan Street. Tel: 03 442 8059. Open: daily 9am–7.30pm summer; 9am–5pm winter. Admission charge.*

### MOTOR MUSEUM
Over 80 well-preserved classic cars and motorcycles make up this historic collection.
*Brecon Street. Tel: 03 442 8775. Open: daily 9.30am–5.30pm. Admission charge.*

### SKYLINE GONDOLA AND KIWI MAGIC
A good way to orientate yourself when you first arrive is to take the Skyline Gondola, which rises 450m from central Queenstown to give stunning views of the lake, mountains and town itself from the restaurant/viewing platform at the top of Bob's Peak. In a wide-screen viewing theatre inside the complex there are regular screenings of a short film, *Kiwi Magic*, which takes you on a highly realistic tour by helicopter, jet-boat, biplane, ski-sled and raft through some of New Zealand's most beautiful scenery.
*Brecon Street. Tel: 03 442 7680. Open: daily 9am–midnight. Admission charge.*
Kiwi Magic *is screened on the hour, 11am–9pm. Admission charge.*

### TSS *EARNSLAW* AND WALTER PEAK FARM
The 80-year-old TSS *Earnslaw* is the last of the coal-burning steamers that once plied the lake to supply outlying sheep stations; lovingly restored, the venerable steamer now cruises for pleasure only. In the afternoons the steamer calls in at Walter Peak, a high-country farm on the other side of the lake, where refreshments are served and sheepdog and sheep-shearing demonstrations are given.
*TSS* Earnslaw *is operated by Fiordland Travel, 4–14 Steamer Wharf (tel: 03 442 7500). Cruises depart three times daily, with barbecue lunch options on several departures. Walter Peak can also be visited by launch at other times (bookings through Fiordland Travel).*

## STEWART ISLAND

This triangular-shaped island is a naturalist's paradise. The figures speak for themselves: 172,000 hectares of native bush and rain forest, nearly 90 per cent of which is protected; 750km of indented coastline with hundreds of hidden beaches and sandy bays; and a mere 20km of roads! There is just one township, Halfmoon Bay (Oban), and a permanent population of only 400 people.

Stewart Island has a rich Maori history, and the harvesting of *titi* (fledgling chicks of the sooty sheerwater) continues on the tiny islands around its coastline as it has done for centuries.

Cook sailed around the southern tip in March 1770, but mistakenly thought it was a peninsula. Twenty years later Captain Chase on board the *Pegasus* brought a sealing gang to these shores and attempted to set up a shipyard on an inlet on the southeast coast (still named Port Pegasus); the island was named after his first officer, William Stewart, who charted the inlet.

Today, commercial fishing – principally for *paua*, crayfish and blue cod – is the lifeblood of most islanders, with tourism now playing an important part as hikers, hunters, divers and fishermen seek out Stewart Island's wild places.

Hikers should arrive well equipped: the North West Circuit (around the top half of the island) takes 10 days, while the Rakiura Track (closer to Oban) takes at least three. Native birds include the kiwi, kaka, tui, bellbird, robin, tomtit, fantail, and long-tailed and shining cuckoo. One of the great attractions of the island is the chance to see kiwis in their natural habitat – unusually, the Stewart Island brown kiwi forages during the daytime (they are particularly numerous at Mason Bay on the North West Circuit). Launch trips also depart from Oban to watch kiwis foraging for sand-hoppers on Ocean Beach during the evenings.

*Stewart Island can be reached on a 20-minute flight (up to four times daily) with Southern Air from Invercargill. Tel: 03 218 9129; toll free: 0800 843 475. There is also a 60-minute catamaran service, the Foveaux Express, from Bluff. Tel: 03 212 7660. Kiwi-watching trips are operated every second night by Bravo Adventure Cruises, Stewart Island. Tel: 03 219 1144 (book far in advance).*

## TE ANAU

See pages 130–1.

## WANAKA

This more laid-back version of Queenstown is set in similarly stunning scenery on the edge of Lake Wanaka, with the peaks of the Mount Aspiring National Park rising up in the background. Wanaka's waterfront is at its most majestic in the autumn, when poplars and willows in shades of gold and red frame the alpine views.

Although less commercialised than Queenstown, outdoor adventure is still the main business here and there is no shortage of thrills on offer, from paragliding to rafting, mountain-biking, jet-boating, four-wheel-drive tours and cruising on the lake by hovercraft. For something even more unusual, you can take a ride in a vintage Tiger Moth biplane. Naturally enough, Wanaka is a major fishing centre, and both coarse fishing on the lake and fly fishing on nearby rivers are available. Hikers are also well catered for as numerous tracks run through the Mount Aspiring National Park; shorter walks in the vicinity include the Diamond Lake Track

You could spend ages trying to find your way out of this maze in Wanaka

(2½ hours) and Mount Roy Track (5–6 hours return). In the winter, skiers head for the renowned Cardrona and Treble Cone ski fields.

For a gentler form of entertainment, don't miss the Stuart Landsborough's Puzzling World and Great Maze; built in 1973, it started a trend which led to the creation of numerous mazes throughout New Zealand. The split-level maze has over 1.5km of passageways, whilst the Tilted Towers complex will confuse you even further. Next to the tea-rooms is the Puzzle Centre, housing a huge collection of mind-bending puzzles and the Illusions Gallery.

*Details on activities are available from the visitor centre, Ardmore Street. Tel: 03 443 1233. Hiking information is available from the DOC informaton centre in the visitor centre building. Tel: 03 443 7660. Tiger Moth scenic and stunt flights are operated by Biplane Adventures, PO Box 262, Wanaka. Tel: 03 443 1000.*

*Stuart Landsborough's Puzzling World and Great Maze, Main Highway, 2km outside town on SH8A to Cromwell. Tel: 03 443 7489. Open: daily 8.30am–5.30pm. Admission charge.*

*120km north of Queenstown (recommended route via Cromwell; extra care is necessary if using Crown Range road during the winter months).*

# Otago Peninsula

This tour around the peninsula is a wildlife extravaganza of sea birds and marinelife, with a historic castle thrown in for good measure. Ideally, you should plan to arrive at the Royal Albatross Colony between noon and 2pm; book your tour before leaving Dunedin, and also make sure you are booked into the Penguin Place Yellow-Eyed Penguin Conservation Reserve for the 4pm tour (see details opposite). *Allow a full day.*

*From the Octagon, head down Princes Street and take a left turn down Andersons Bay Road. After 5km, turn left down Silverton Road and follow the signs to Larnach Castle (see page 133) along the ridgetop road. After visiting Larnach return to the Highcliff Road and turn left, continuing down to Hoopers Inlet and then following Sheppard Road to the Papanui Inlet.*

## *1* HOOPERS AND PAPANUI INLETS

Both of these lovely inlets are home to a variety of wading and water birds. The innermost part of Hoopers Inlet is a wildlife sanctuary – a plaque by the roadside illustrates the birds that can be seen here at different times of year.

*Take Weir Road to Portobello Bay and continue along the coast road, stopping at Southlight Wildlife to collect the key for the reserve itself. Continue on to Taiaroa Head.*

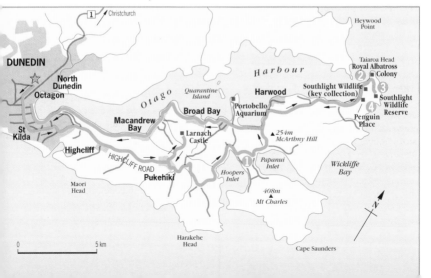

A Royal Albatross at Taiaroa Head on the tip of the peninsula

## *2* ROYAL ALBATROSS COLONY

This reserve is one of the most special wildlife zones in New Zealand, and the only mainland albatross colony of its kind in the world. The area has been protected since 1937, and public viewing started in 1972. The Albatross Centre has displays and an audio-visual presentation on these magnificent birds, and from here you are led by trained guides up to the hide overlooking the nesting sites on the hilltop.

Winging in from Antarctic waters, the albatross build their nests in late September and, once all the eggs have been laid (usually by 24 November), the colony is open to the public. The tasks of incubation and guarding the new-born chicks are shared by both parents, with hatching taking place between January and February. The massive, fluffy albatross chicks remain at Taiaroa until they are ready to set off in late September.

*Continue past the car-park, through the gate and along the clifftop road to Southlight Wildlife Reserve.*

## *3* SOUTHLIGHT WILDLIFE RESERVE

Yellow-eyed penguins come ashore in the late afternoons to nest above the beach here, but you won't get as close to them as you will in the Penguin Place Reserve. However, there are plenty of fur seals to photograph at close quarters, and at the end of the beach is a spotted shag colony.

*Return along the coast road to Penguin Place. If you have time, you could also detour back to the Portobello Aquarium (see page 133).*

## *4* PENGUIN PLACE YELLOW-EYED PENGUIN CONSERVATION RESERVE

This is by far the better of the two penguin reserves. After a brief introductory talk at the farm headquarters, you are ferried over the hill to the penguin beach where a series of crafty tunnels and hides allows you to pop up within a metre or two of the many nesting sites in this colony.

*Return to Dunedin around the shoreline.*

**Royal Albatross Colony**, PO Box 492, Dunedin (reservations essential, tel: 03 478 0499). Open: daily 9am–dusk. Tours operate on the hour and half-hour. Admission charge.
**Southlight Wildlife**, Harington Point (tel: 03 478 0287). Open: daily dawn–dusk. Admission charge.
**Penguin Place Yellow-eyed Penguin Conservation Reserve**, PO Box 963 (tel: 03 478 0286). Open: daily 9am–dusk. Admission charge.

# Milford Sound

This tour starts and finishes in Te Anau, following the Milford Road with several interesting stop-offs before arriving at Milford itself, where you have a choice of cruise options on the sound. If you are based in Queenstown it is better to do the trip by coach or cruise excursion so that someone else drives the six hours involved. *Allow a full day to complete the tour at a leisurely pace.*

*From Te Anau, follow signs for Milford Sound.*

## 1 LAKE TE ANAU

The road skirts Lake Te Anau, with views across to the Murchison Mountains, before arriving at Te Anau Downs and then heading away from the lake up towards the Livingstone and Humboldt mountains.

*At the 40km mark you pass the entrance to the Fiordland National Park; after 58km you arrive at the Mirror Lakes.*

## 2 MIRROR LAKES

A boardwalk from the road leads around the edge of two small, sheltered lakes which mirror the mountains opposite – hundreds of day-trippers pour off their tour buses to capture this famous scene on film. Shortly afterwards, you drive along the Avenue of the Disappearing Mountain, so called because the peak at the end of the road seems to diminish in perspective the closer you get to it.

*At 76km, the road skirts Lake Gunn.*

## 3 LAKE GUNN

Lake Gunn sometimes also has a mirror image of the mountains, although less reliably so than the Mirror Lakes. This large lake is named after an early explorer, George Gunn. From the road a loop track leads through red beech forest to the lakeside (a pleasant half-hour's

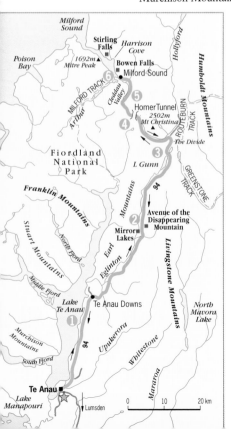

ramble). Shortly afterwards you pass The Divide, the lowest east–west pass (534m) across the Southern Alps and the departure point for the Routeburn and Greenstone tracks.
*Continue on to the Homer Tunnel (101km).*

### 4 HOMER TUNNEL

The tunnel was started in 1935 when just five men set to the mountain with picks and shovels; not surprisingly, it wasn't completed until 1952, and at the cost of five lives. Hewn out of solid rock, the tunnel is narrow and unlined, dropping along a gradient of one in 11 over its 1.2km length. You can't help but drive through with extreme caution.

### 5 CLEDDAU VALLEY

As the road emerges from the Homer Tunnel it spirals down the Cleddau Valley, with dozens of waterfalls tumbling over the sheer sides of the valley.

Dramatic scenery in the Milford Sound

Further down, the Cleddau river plunges beneath a natural rock bridge to create another spectacular waterfall.
*At the 120km point you arrive at Milford Sound, from where cruises depart down the Sound to the Tasman Sea. A visitor centre with facilities is available.*

### 6 MILFORD SOUND

The rainfall is practically incessant in Milford Sound (averaging over 6,200mm per year), giving it an almost permanent misty, moody atmosphere and contributing to the dozens of spectacular but temporary waterfalls that tumble down the sheer rock faces into the sea. Most cruises take a similar route down the 16km-long sound, first passing by Mitre Peak (1,692m) and then nosing in for a spray-filled view of Bowen Falls before nearing a fur seal colony and heading up to the Tasman Sea. On the return journey, your captain will point out hanging glacial valleys and other features, and will try to seek out schools of dolphins. The boat passes the wind-lashed Stirling Falls, Harrison Cove and, once again, the Bowen Falls before docking back at the visitor centre jetty.
*Return to Te Anau along the same route.*

# The Routeburn Track

This is one of New Zealand's great walks, a relatively easy, well-marked track passing from the Fiordland National Park over the Harris Saddle and into the Mount Aspiring National Park. It is a popular route, with spectacular alpine panoramas along much of its 39km length. The track can be walked independently in either direction or on a guided tramp from west to east, as described here. For practical details, see page 144. *Allow three days.*

*Your trek begins with a coach ride from Queenstown, through Te Anau and along the Milford Highway to The Divide, from where you start walking.*

## 1 DAY ONE: THE DIVIDE TO LAKE MACKENZIE

The track climbs gently through magnificent silver-beech forests, with the gnarled trunks of the larger trees draped in a cloak of mosses, lichens and epiphytes. Once you emerge above the tree-line, you detour briefly up to Key Summit (919m), a small rocky knoll surrounded by a swampland of bogs and tarns, with extensive views of the peaks and valleys of Fiordland. From here it is a quick descent to Lake Howden, where there is time for lunch. The afternoon's walk is a steady but gentle climb from Lake Howden to Lake Mackenzie, passing the dramatic Earland Falls on the way. The track goes almost directly underneath these 100m-high falls, and the surrounding rocks and ferns are drenched in spray. Further along, there are occasional glimpses of the snow-capped peaks and glaciers of the Darren Range. A last, rocky descent through silver-beech forest comes out at the Mackenzie Hut, where you stop for the night.

The Routeburn Track offers spectacular mountain views, such as this panorama of the Darren Range

## 2 DAY TWO: LAKE MACKENZIE TO ROUTEBURN FALLS

After breakfast you set off alongside Lake Mackenzie, which on a calm day will reward you with a breath-taking image of Emily Peak (1,820m) reflected in its emerald depths. The track zigzags steeply up above the tree-line before levelling out and hugging the Hollyford Face for the next two to three hours; from here there are magnificent views across the valley to the Darren Range. A brief ascent brings you to the Harris Saddle (1,217m), where you pass from the Fiordland National Park into the Mount Aspiring National Park.

From the shelter at Harris Saddle it is well worth making the extra effort to climb Conical Hill (1,515m). There are awe-inspiring views from its summit of the Hollyford Valley leading down to Lake McKerrow, Martins Bay and the Tasman Sea.

Beyond Harris Saddle the track skirts Lake Harris, emerging into the fragile tussock and swampland of the Harris Basin. The track then follows the Routeburn river down to the Routeburn Falls, well known as a haunt for mischievous keas. Your hut for the night is within earshot of the falls.

## 3 DAY THREE: ROUTEBURN FALLS TO ROUTEBURN SHELTER

The track descends through silver-, mountain- and then red-beech forest. At the Routeburn Flats, the river winds placidly across the grass-covered plains, with Mount Somnus (2,294m) dominating the view. After you have crossed the Routeburn on a suspension bridge, a gentle downhill amble along the river's forested banks leads you to the Routeburn Shelter, from where you will be transported back to Queenstown.

# The Routeburn Track

## Weather and hazards

The Routeburn is a well-used and clearly marked path, with tracks, huts and bridges maintained efficiently by park staff. Most people walk the track during the summer months (mid-November to March), although autumn (April to mid-May) can also be excellent, with less people on the trail. Mountain flowers are at their best from November to January. Rainfall can be high during midsummer, so the best views are often to be had from February to April. The main hazard is the southerly or northwesterly storms which come in from the Tasman Sea, and which can occur at any time of year. The answer is to be prepared for adverse conditions with waterproofs and warm clothing.

The Routeburn Track is one of the most popular walks in the South Island

## Guided walks

Guided walking is a comfortable and pleasant option which allows anybody of average fitness to enjoy this wonderful area, even if they have had no previous hiking experience. Routeburn Walk Ltd has its own private mountain lodges with comfortable accommodation and hot showers. All meals are prepared by the guides and the lodge managers, which means that during the day you have only to carry a light day pack with your clothing and other requirements. The friendly and knowledgeable guides will ensure a safe journey and allow you to make the most of this superb walk.

*For full details on costs and bookings, contact: Routeburn Walk, PO Box 568, Queenstown (tel: 03 442 8200; toll free: 0800 659 255). Departures: January to March, daily; November, December and April, weekdays only.*

## Independent walking

Public transport is available from both ends of the track, and hut wardens are in residence from November to May. *Maps and information can be obtained from the Fiordland National Park Visitor Centre, PO Box 29, Te Anau (tel: 03 249 7921). Open: daily from 8am in summer, 9am in winter (call for closing times), or the DOC office, Oban Street, Glenorchy. Tel: 03 442 9937. Open: November to April, daily 8.30am–5pm (weekdays only in winter).*

# GETTING AWAY FROM IT ALL

'Compared to England it is like
the week after a bloodless and
smiling revolution.'

**J B PRIESTLEY**
*A Visit to New Zealand, 1974*

# Getting Away From it All

*M*any people come to New Zealand specifically for its wide open spaces and unspoiled natural environment, and since New Zealanders themselves are equally keen on the great outdoors there is no shortage of opportunities to get away from it all. The activities listed here form just a sample of the options available (see also pages 162–5), but they can be enjoyed by anyone and are, in their own way, typically Kiwi ways to escape – whether only for a few seconds on a bungee jump or several days on a rafting or walking trip.

## BALLOONING
Canterbury Plains is the biggest centre for hot-air ballooning in New Zealand, thanks largely to the rolling countryside

which provides ideal conditions for drifting quietly along high above the sheep and farmlands below. The scenery is spectacular, with the Southern Alps rearing up to the west and the Pacific coastline stretching off into the distance to the east. Most balloon flights start at dawn (to take advantage of calm conditions), but the trauma of having to get up so early is soon forgotten in the excitement of clambering into the basket and lifting off. After the initial roar of the gas burners you can settle back to enjoy your hour-long flight. Champagne is always served on landing (a tradition with balloonists worldwide), followed by a hearty breakfast.

**Aoraki Balloon Safaris**, Methven (tel: 03 302 8172).

**High Country Ballooning**, The MacKenzie Basin, Twizel (tel: 03 435 0100).

**Up, Up, and Away**, PO Box 36014, Christchurch (tel: 03 355 7141).

## BUNGEE-JUMPING
Jumping off high places with nothing but a piece of elastic tied to your ankles is perhaps one of the oddest adventure sports ever invented, but at least 70,000 people a year are now taking the plunge. The attraction lies partly in conquering your inner fears sufficiently to throw yourself off, partly in the exhilaration of

the 'drop', and partly in the relief that floods through you as the bungee cord drags you back up again and you bounce gently in mid-air before being hoisted aboard a raft on the river below.

Bungee-jumping was invented by a New Zealander, A J Hackett and started as a commercial operation in Queenstown in 1988 with the Kawarau Bridge jump (43m). You can now also jump at the Skippers Canyon Suspension Bridge (71m) and at other locations such as Lake Taupo. It is surprising how many people come back for more, and there is no age limit either – over-65s go free, and the oldest person ever to have jumped was 89. The whole organisation is highly professional (the sport has an excellent safety record), and motorised cameras and videos capture your jump on film so that you can astound your friends later.

Going down is easy – it's the steps back up that are hard work. A bungee-jumper high above the Kawarau River

**A J Hackett Bungy,** Shotover Street, Queenstown (tel: 03 442 7100; toll free: 0800 105 550). Bookings essential.

## JET-BOATING

Jet-boats were invented by the Kiwi engineer and farmer, Bill Hamilton, to operate on the shallow and otherwise unnavigable rivers of the South Island. Unlike normal boats, the propeller on the jet-boat is on the inside of the hull, driving water out through a nozzle at the rear with tremendous force. The nozzle also steers the boat, giving it incredible manoeuvrability – jet-boats can execute high-speed, 360-degree turns almost on their own axis. High-speed 'jet-spins', 'flick turns' and other manoeuvres provide thrills and excitement for the majority of passengers on rivers such as the Shotover and Kawarau, but the real benefit of jet-boats is that they can venture far into the wilderness up shallow river systems as they can operate in just 10cm of water. If you can, take a jet-boat safari up through the beautiful Dart River Valley or somewhere similarly remote; you will find jet-boats for hire at many riverside localities throughout the country.

**Dart River Jetboat Safari,** Box 76, Queenstown (tel: 03 442 9992).
**Huka Jet,** PO Box 563, Taupo (tel: 07 374 8572).
**Shotover Jet,** Arthurs Point, Queenstown (tel: 03 442 8570).

# Walking

*T*here is no better way to experience New Zealand's wild and beautiful back-country than by spending a few days walking on one of the many long-distance tracks that traverse the country. Forests, mountains, lakes, beaches, volcanoes – each track has its own special characteristics, most taking two to five days to complete. Tramping, as its called in New Zealand, is one of the most popular (and certainly one of the best value) activities for getting away from it all. The network encompasses over 100 tramping tracks, although most visitors opt for one of the four main tracks listed below. The best season for walking runs from October to March.

### Abel Tasman

Rated the easiest tramp of its length in New Zealand, this is a good choice if you have never tramped before and want to give it a go. The track is well marked and well graded – almost a gentle amble – and passes beach after beach along a seashore backed by native forests. This is considered to be one of the most beautiful coastal walks in the world, through an area renowned for its mild, sunny weather. Not surprisingly, it is the most popular track in the country; boats also ferry walkers between the beaches.
*50km, three to four days. Marahau to Totaranui or Wainui, or vice versa. Easy. Daily bus connections to/from Nelson.*

### Kepler

This is the newest and certainly the best-planned tramping track in New Zealand, and was designed to take the pressure off other Fiordland tramps; as a result, the Kepler has become a classic in its own right. The track follows a circular route, passing through stunning alpine landscapes of lakes, mountains and beech forests. Steep gradients make this a tougher walk than the Routeburn or the Milford.
*67km, four days. Start and finish near Te Anau. Difficult.*

### Milford

This is New Zealand's best-known track, and for this reason is the only one that requires pre-booked hut accommodation. Although highly regulated (you can only walk in one direction, and must complete it in the time alloted, so there are no breaks for bad weather), the walk is still worth doing for its spectacular views of alpine meadows, forests and waterfalls – including Sutherland Falls, the highest in the country at 580m. Although the track can be rough in places, it is within the capabilities of the averagely fit.
*53km, three to six days. Lake Te Anau to Milford Sound. Medium.*
*It is essential to book well in advance during the peak summer months: DOC, PO Box 29, Te Anau (tel: 03 249 8514).*

**Routeburn**, see pages 142–3.
*39km, three to four days. Lake Wakatipu to Upper Hollyford Valley, or vice versa. Medium.*

### OTHER MAJOR TRACKS

The most frequently used tracks in the North Island are the Tongariro Crossing in the Tongariro National Park, the shoreline track around Lake Waikaremoana and the Coromandel

State Forest Park Walk. Popular tracks in the South Island, include the Heaphy and Wangapeka in the North-West Nelson Forest Park (which comes within the Kahurangi National Park), the Travers-Sabine Circuit in the Nelson Lakes National Park, and the Rees-Dart, Hollyford, and Greenstone-Caples Tracks in Fiordland. The Northern Circuit/Rakiura Track on Stewart Island is also classified as one of the 'great walks'.

## INDEPENDENT TRAMPING

Your first stop for information should be the Department of Conservation (DOC) information centres. The DOC maintains thousands of kilometres of tracks and over 900 huts, as well as publishing a number of useful brochures, including 'The World at Your Feet – Tramping in the New Zealand Backcountry' and 'Exploring New Zealand's Parks', plus individual brochures on most tramping tracks. *Head Office, DOC, PO Box 10–420, Wellington (tel: 04 471 0726).*

## GUIDED TRAMPING

If you are not used to carrying a large backpack for several days, a guided tramp allows you to experience some tracks by staying in privately owned, comfortable huts en route and carrying just a day pack. Such tramps are more costly than going it alone, but may suit inexperienced or more elderly walkers.

**Milford Track Guided Walk**, PO Box 185, Te Anau (tel: 03 249 7411 and toll-free 0800 659 255).

**Routeburn Guided Walk and Greenstone-Caples Guided Walk**, PO Box 568, Queenstown (tel: 03 442 8200).

Tramping is almost a national pastime, and facilities are well organised

# White-water Rafting

Given the number of rivers and rapids in New Zealand, it is hardly surprising that rafting is one of the most popular outdoor adventures for visitors. There are more than 50 rafting companies in the country, which between them offer a wide range of trips to suit everyone from beginners to more experienced rafters looking for wild and wet adventures. The season usually runs from late October to March, although many trips now operate year round, rafters simply donning thicker wetsuits.

Queenstown is the main focus of rafting in the South Island, with half-day trips available on the nearby Shotover and Kawarau rivers, and two-day

The thrills and spills of white-water rafting are open to everyone

expeditions to the beautiful Landsborough river which flows through deep gorges from its source in the Mount Cook National Park. The Buller, Clarence, Waimakariri, Rakaia and Rangitata are other well-known rafting rivers in the South Island. The most challenging white-water rafting in the South Island is on the Karamea, a Grade 5 river which runs down from the Tasman Mountains in Nelson; you need a helicopter to get to the start-point.

In the North Island most rafting takes place on the Mohaka, Rangataiki, Rangitikei and Motu rivers. The Wairoa is also popular, although its Grade 5 ride is only possible on 26 days of the year as the river is controlled by hydroelectric schemes. The ultimate rafting sensation in the Rotorua area is the upper Kaituna river (grade 5+), which drops 7m over Hinemoa's Steps – the highest commercially rafted waterfall in the world.

**Buller Adventure Tours**
Half-day tours on the Buller and full- or three-day adventures on the Karamea (including helicopter flight).
*Buller Gorge Road, Westport (tel: 03 789 7286).*

**Raging Thunder**
Long-established and highly experienced operator; wide variety of raft trips (including the Landsborough).
*Shotover and Camp streets, Queenstown (tel: 03 442 7318).*

**River Rats**
One of the largest North Island rafting companies, wide choice of rivers, including the Kaituna.
*PO Box 90 232, Auckland (tel: 09 309 2211).*

# DIRECTORY

'There is nothing soft about New Zealand,
the country. It is very hard and sinewy, and will
outlast many of those who try to alter it.'
**JOHN MULGAN,**
*Report on Experience,* 1947

# Shopping

$N$ew Zealand is not renowned for bargain shopping. While there are locally produced goods of excellent quality, these can be fairly pricey: a recent survey showed that thousands of tourists were leaving the country with money still in their wallets because the things they wanted to buy were too expensive. So, be warned that you may have to dig deep for that coveted item. The best buys are sheepskin, crafts and greenstone. For shop opening times, see page 185–6.

## WHAT TO BUY
### Arts and crafts

Craftspeople seem to thrive in New Zealand, and if you like hand-crafted items you will be spoilt for choice. Many souvenir shops stock handicrafts, but you can find better bargains by buying directly from studios. In major craft centres such as Nelson, Golden Bay and the Coromandel you can pick up 'Craft Trail' leaflets listing the locations, opening times and specialities of local studios.

Pottery and woodcarvings are perhaps the most widely available products, although you can also find glassware, hand-weaving, metalwork, patchwork, wooden toys, jewellery, bone-carvings, decorative boxes and much more. Traditional and contemporary Maori woodcarvings are also widely available.

Jewellery and other souvenirs made from iridescent *paua* (abalone) shell are also worth looking at. In comparison to elsewhere in the world, greenstone or jade is excellent value, particularly smaller items such as finely carved *tiki* good-luck charms. Larger sculpted pieces, which may take many months to work, can run into thousands of dollars.

A craftsman in Hokitika working a large piece of greenstone

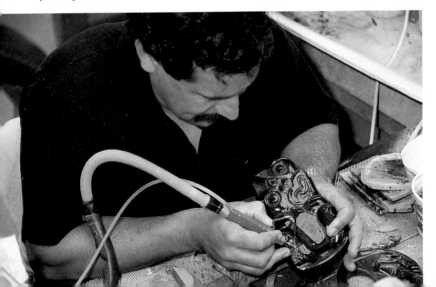

Pendants and other greenstone jewellery are popular souvenirs

### Clothing and sheepskin

Rugged outdoor clothing (such as jackets and bushwacker hats) is worth looking at, particularly classic designs made with deerskin, sheepskin, leather or suede. Hand-knitted sweaters and other woollen items are expensive but worth splashing out on.

One of the best known labels for leisurewear is Canterbury of New Zealand, whose colourful, all-cotton rugby shirts are a good buy; other good-quality brands include Jackson Bay, Action Down Under, T&Ski and MacKenzie Country Knitwear.

Sheepskin is turned into everything from bedroom slippers to car seat covers and floor rugs; the leading manufacturer is Bowron. Lambskin, luxuriously soft since it has only been shorn once, is particularly popular.

### Other specialities

Wines, cheeses, pre-packed Bluff oysters and honey scented with native flowers are further options if you want to take home a taste of New Zealand. CDs and cassettes of Maori songs make an appealing souvenir, and are usually sold at Maori concerts as well as record and souvenir shops.

# Where to Shop

## NORTH ISLAND
### AUCKLAND
**Auckland Museum**

Excellent quality Maori arts and crafts, as well as jewellery and other well-designed souvenirs. Good selection of Maori CDs and tapes.

*The Domain (tel: 09 309 0443). Open: daily 10am–5pm.*

**Parnell**

Probably the best up-market shopping area in Auckland, with dozens of high-quality craft shops, art galleries, antique shops and fashion boutiques that spread out into the streets surrounding the quaint shopping arcade known as Parnell Village.

*Parnell Street and environs.*

**Queen Street**

Auckland's main shopping street, with a mix of department stores, fashion outlets, souvenir shops and jewellers. The side streets on the east side (such as High Street and Vulcan Lane) are worth a look, with interesting bookshops, boutiques and cafés.

**Victoria Park Market**

Has a good selection of off-beat arts and crafts, as well as T-shirts and reasonably priced leather and sheepskin goods.

*Victoria Street West and corner of Wellesley Street (tel: 09 309 6911). Open: Monday to Saturday 9am–7pm, Sunday 10am–7pm.*

### ROTORUA

As one of the country's premier tourist destinations, Rotorua has numerous souvenir and duty-free shops.

**Agrodome**

Like Rainbow Springs (opposite), Agrodome is geared towards a huge through-put of package tourists, and all the usual sheepskin, woollen and leather goods can be purchased here.

*Ngongotaha (tel: 07 357 4350). Open: daily 9am–5pm.*

**New Zealand Arts and Crafts Institute**

Authentic hand-crafted Maori carvings from workshops where

Shopping in Parnell Village, Auckland

the traditional styles are taught.
*Hemo Road, Whakarewarewa (tel: 07 348 9047). Open: daily 8.30am–5pm.*

### Rainbow Springs
The recently rebuilt international shopping complex here claims to be the largest souvenir shop in New Zealand, and stocks a huge range of items including knitwear, sheepskin, leather goods, bone- and woodcarvings, and opal and *paua* (abalone shell) jewellery.
*Fairy Springs Road, Auckland Highway (SH5), (tel: 07 347 9301). Open: daily 8am–5pm.*

# SOUTH ISLAND
## CHRISTCHURCH
There is a good selection of shops in central downtown Christchurch, with pedestrianised or enclosed malls radiating outwards from Cathedral Square.

### Arts Centre
The Arts Centre, with its numerous small workshops and galleries, is one of the best places in the South Island for crafts; there is even more choice at the centre's weekend markets.
*Arts Centre, Worcester Street (tel: 03 363 2836). Open: weekdays 8.30am–5pm, weekends 10am–5pm. Market open: weekends 10am–5pm.*

### New Regent Street
One block north of the square (leading off from Gloucester Street) is New Regent Street, a quaint row of pastel-painted shops which formed the first 'shopping mall' in the country when it opened in 1931. Crystals, antiquarian books, fashion and herbal remedies are among the range of goods on offer.

## HOKITIKA
### Jade Boulder Gallery
High-quality, individually designed greenstone (jade) sculptures and jewellery.
*1 Guinness Street (tel: 03 768 0700). Open: weekdays 8.30am–5.30pm, weekends 9am–5pm.*

### Mountain Jade
Exquisite jade carvings, sculptures and jewellery.
*Weld Street (tel: 03 755 8007). Open: daily 8am–5pm.*

### Westland Greenstone
One of the largest processors of greenstone, with a wide range of items available.
*34 Tancred Street (tel: 03 755 8713). Open: daily 8am–5pm.*

## QUEENSTOWN
Queenstown has an excellent range of shops, and is the only place in New Zealand where major stores and boutiques stay open until 10pm, seven days a week. Jewellery, leatherwork and sheepskin shops, and a huge range of fashion and outdoor clothing stores all lie within a few minutes' walk of each other in the pedestrianised streets that run parallel to the Mall in the downtown area.

## WELLINGTON
The main shopping street is Lambton Quay, which has several covered arcades and some small, speciality shops on its north side. Further on, Willis Street, Manners Street and Cuba Street all have a similar mix of shops. A good place to look for crafts, posters, clothes and so on is Wakefield Market (corner of Jervois Quay and Taranaki Street), which is open Fridays, weekends and public holidays. A good area for New Zealand craft souvenirs and jewellery, including antiques and art galleries, is Tinakori Road.

# Entertainment

## AGRICULTURAL SHOWS

This is a farming country, so why not look in on a real agricultural show, which every self-respecting town holds annually? Known as A&P (agricultural and pastoral) shows, these country fairs usually have prize produce and stock on display, competitions for wood-chopping, and all the usual rides and side-shows. Agricultural shows aimed specifically at tourists are, surprisingly, also good fun (see pages 64–5).

## CLASSICAL MUSIC, DANCE AND THEATRE

The main classical orchestras are the New Zealand Symphony Orchestra (based in Wellington) and the Auckland Philharmonic Orchestra, both of which give regular concerts from their home bases and in regional centres. The Royal New Zealand Ballet (based in Wellington) also tours extensively, often with visiting soloists. Despite the existence of talented opera stars such as Dame Kiri Te Kanawa and Dame Malvina Major, grand opera is only staged regionally in the four main centres, but to a high standard. Dame Kiri does, however, sometimes perform at outdoor concerts and other events. Theatre has proliferated in New Zealand, with many professional and semi-professional theatre groups staging productions in the major centres.

## OTHER ENTERTAINMENT

The most internationally renowned pop group to have come out of New Zealand was Split Enz, now disbanded. Plenty of aspiring rock bands do, however, perform on the pub circuit, as do blues, jazz and folk musicians. Auckland, Wellington, Christchurch and Queenstown are the best places for live music, and there are also discos in the major centres.

Most towns and cities have cinemas, with new films shown soon after their international release. Out-of-town multiplex cinemas are also fairly common.

## MAORI CONCERTS

Although most Maori concerts are presented principally for the tourist trade, they still present a genuine example of the culture – indeed, many young Maori have rediscovered their traditions and re-learnt old skills via these shows. They are also highly professional, with many of the concert groups touring overseas. A typical performance will start with a *wero* (challenge), followed by a *powhiri* (welcoming) and a *hongi* (a greeting which involves the touching of noses), all of which are explained. These introductions will then be followed by various songs and dances, such as the *haka* or *poi* (see pages 158–9), usually with some entertaining audience participation. Many concerts are also followed by a *hangi* feast.

Daytime concerts are held at the Auckland Museum (see page 33) and at the Whakarewarewa Thermal Reserve in Rotorua (see page 67). Several large hotels in Rotorua (such as the Sheraton, the Lake Plaza and the THC Rotorua Hotel) put on evening concerts, but by far the best way to experience Maori culture is to go to a concert and *hangi* held on a *marae*, where you will get a much more authentic feel for the culture. These are run by the following Maori groups:

One of many cultural events, festivals and concerts staged throughout the year

**Tamaki Tours**, PO Box 1492, Rotorua (tel: 07 346 2823).
**Magic of the Maori**, 51 Lake Road, Ohinemutu, Rotorua Tel: 07 349 3949. Freephone 0508 300 333.

## EVENTS
New Zealand stages a huge range of events and cultural activities each year, from gumboot-throwing competitions to internationally acclaimed arts festivals. The best source of information is the annual '*Special Events*' brochure produced by the tourism board. Some of the regular annual events include the following:
### January
Annual yachting regatta, Auckland.
Summer City Mardi Gras, Wellington.
### February
Treaty of Waitangi Celebrations, Bay of Islands.
Wine and Food Festival, Christchurch; Blenheim (Marlborough) and Martinborough (Wairarapa).
NZ International Festival of the Arts, Wellington (biennial – even years).
### March
Golden Shears International Sheep Shearing Championships, Masterton.

Ngaruawahia River Regatta for Maori Canoes, Waikato River.
Wild & Wacky Adventure Sports Festival, Christchurch.
International Billfish Tournament, Bay of Islands.
### April
Round the Bays Fun Run, Wellington and Auckland.
NZ Easter Show and Festival, Auckland.
### June
Auckland Winter Festival.
International Car Rally, Auckland.
### July
Auckland Film Festival
Canterbury Winter Carnival, Christchurch.
### September
The Great NZ Craft Show, Christchurch.
Annual Citrus Festival, Te Puke.
### October
Labour Day.
World Festival of Golf, Canterbury.
### November
Cup Carnival Week, Christchurch.
Rhododendron Festival, Taranaki.
### December
Summertime Festival, Christchurch.

# MAORI ARTS, CRAFTS AND

## Weaving and tattoos

The early Maori used seal and dog skins to stay warm in Aotearoa's relatively cool climate, but, more importantly, they developed the use of flax as the main source of material for clothing. Flax fibres were twisted into patterns to create fabrics, a form of hand-weaving that produced exceptionally fine work; cloaks were also decorated with feathers, dyed strands or fur.

Tattooing (*moko*) was an important part of an individual's identity and status, and warriors would often be tattooed not only all over their faces but on their thighs and buttocks as well. Women's tattoos extended only up to the chin. The process was long and extremely painful, with designs actually cut into the flesh with a chisel before soot was rubbed into the pattern.

## Carving

Carving was used to decorate almost everything from adze handles to musical instruments, and master carvers enjoyed high status in the community. Carving reached its highest form in the decoration of *whare runanga* (meeting-houses) and food storage houses.

The most common motifs are the *manaia* (a bird-like, half-human figure) and *hei-tiki*. Usually called simply *tiki*, the significance of the latter, small figurines that are sold widely today as charms, has now been lost.

## Music and dance

Dance was an integral feature of Maori life, signalling important events or ceremonial occasions within the tribe. Traditionally, songs and dances were accompanied by flutes (made from whalebone and wood), and, as drums were unknown, the rhythm was marked only by foot stomping and the slapping of hands on the chest and thighs.

Maori cultural heritage includes superb carvings and animated song and dance

# DANCE

Later, Maori also took to the guitar and adapted Victorian melodies to their own poetic songs.

*Haka* is a generic term applied to all rhythmic dances, although today it is usually applied to the vigorous, shouted dances performed by men, such as the *haka taparahi* and the *peruperu* (war dance). The latter is characterised by the fearsome facial gestures of staring eyes and a protruding tongue, this signalling to potential enemies 'you look good, and I am going to eat you!' The national rugby football team, the All Blacks, uses *haka* choruses to great effect at the start of international matches. The intricate *poi* dance, in which flax balls attached to string are swirled in time to music, is performed only by women.

# Children

New Zealand is in many ways a family-oriented country, and children will be made to feel welcome almost everywhere. There are no problems with language, strange food or culture shock, and no dangerous animals or poisonous insects! Adequate protection from the sun is absolutely essential as New Zealand has high levels of damaging ultraviolet rays. Supplies of baby foods, nappies and other essentials are widely available, and the water is clean and safe to drink everywhere. There are plenty of parks and playgrounds where children can run wild, and as well as enjoying purpose-built attractions such as fun-fairs (the biggest are Fantasyland in Hastings and Rainbow's End in Auckland), they will be enthralled by some of the country's natural wonders, such as volcanoes, glaciers, and bubbling, smelly mud pools.

## ADVENTURE SPORTS

Older children will enjoy adventure sports such as sea kayaking and river rafting, and some companies offer family discounts. Jet-boating is perfectly safe for kids of any age, and, if you can afford it, a helicopter ride will no doubt prove to be a highlight of the trip. The youngest person ever to bungee jump off the Kawaru Bridge near Queenstown was only seven! Unless you have considerable experience, hiking with children is not advisable, although you could certainly walk short sections of the Abel Tasman Coastal Track, where there are regular boat shuttles to and from various beaches. There are plenty of short bush walks and nature trails all over the country.

Riding a big bull at Walter Peak Station, near Queenstown, is quite an experience

## BOAT TRIPS

Scenic cruises are very popular. There is a huge choice of such cruises, from old sailing ships in the Bay of Islands to catamarans on the Marlborough Sounds and old steamships on Lakes Taupo, Rotorua and Wakatipu. Many single-day yacht charters from Auckland include stops for swimming, snorkelling and beach picnics.

## MUSEUMS AND SCIENCE CENTRES

New Zealand has some exceptionally well-designed museum exhibits which make the past come alive in an entertaining way. The Time Tunnel at the top of the Mount Cavendish Gondola in Christchurch, for instance, has volcanoes that blast hot air and a below-decks scene in an immigrant ship that even smells realistic; the Hobson Wharf National Maritime Museum in Auckland also has a convincing mock-up of a ship's interior.

Other top spots for children include: Kelly Tarlton's Antarctic Encounter and Underwater World (Auckland); the International Antarctic Centre (Christchurch); and there is plenty to see at Air Force World (Christchurch) and at the Museum of Transport Technology and Social History (Auckland). But by far the best and most innovative of such centres in New Zealand is Capital Discovery Place (Wellington).

The Museum of New Zealand/Te Papa Tongarewa is the country's first national museum and covers every aspect of New Zealand's life – past, present and future.

## SWIMMING

There are opportunities for swimming in the ocean, rivers and lakes almost everywhere, as well as in swimming-pools

Children's farms are a feature of many zoos

in most major towns and cities. Swimming outdoors is, however, only practicable from late October to early March – except in the north. Not all beaches are safe for swimming, and you should always check locally for hazardous conditions. Surf life-savers operate patrols at popular beaches during the summer. If children spend too long near lakeshores in the summer months they may develop 'duck itch', an unpleasant but harmless irritation caused by a parasite that is carried by ducks.

## WILDLIFE

There are numerous opportunities for getting close to wildlife, particularly on the east coast of the South Island where seal and penguin colonies can be reached after just a short walk. Whale-watching (in Kaikoura) or swimming with dolphins (Bay of Islands and Whakatane) will provide memorable experiences. Most wildlife centres have nocturnal houses where kiwis can be spotted, and if native bird aviaries don't appeal then there are always bigger, more exotic animals in places such as Auckland Zoo, Wellington Zoo and the Orana Park Wildlife Trust (Christchurch), which also have children's farms.

# Sport

New Zealand is a nation of sports and fitness fanatics, with more than 35 per cent of the population belonging to a sporting club of some kind. National teams and individual competitors are followed with considerable pride, and television coverage of sport is extensive. The country has no less than five museums devoted entirely to sport!

## COMPETITIVE SPORTS

Rugby football is the most popular sport in the country, with over 240,000 registered players and many more supporters. The national team, the All Blacks, is held in high esteem (the team-members are probably better known to most New Zealanders than elected politicians) and its progress in international matches is followed avidly.

During the winter, netball (a sport in which New Zealand has several times been world champion), soccer and

hockey are also played. During the summer months, cricket takes over from rugby as the focus of national aspirations abroad. Lawn bowls is incredibly popular, far outstripping other sports such as tennis, squash, softball and basketball.

New Zealanders are also passionate about horse-racing; over 70 tracks around the country feature 'the gallops' by day and 'the trots' by night.

## CYCLING

With its scenic attractions and uncrowded roads, New Zealand is ideal for cycling – but be warned, distances between destinations can be considerable and, of course, the country is also fairly mountainous. If you are heading into the hills or off the beaten track, a mountain bike is essential for the unmetalled side-roads. There are, as yet, very few dedicated off-road routes. Several local cycle-touring guidebooks are available if you want to go it alone, or you can join a group tour with accommodation (or tents) and meals provided, and with a mini-bus back-up. Mountain bikes can be hired in many resort areas.
**Adventure South**, PO Box 33–153, Christchurch (tel: 03 332 1222).
**Mountain Bike Adventure Company**, (tel: 03 384 0006).

New Zealand has some of the best fly fishing in the world on its numerous lakes and rivers

Horse-riding is a great way to enjoy the countryside

**Adventure Cycles**, (tel:09 309 5566).

## FISHING

The many unpolluted rivers and miles of accessible, clean coastline made New Zealand a fisherman's mecca. Licences for inland fisheries are available from fishing-tackle and sports shops for daily, weekly or monthly periods; sea fishing requires no licence. A special tourist licence, valid for the whole of the country for one month, is also available.

The introduction of trout and other species such as salmon and perch has given New Zealand some of the best dry-fly fishing in the world, and reputable and experienced fishing guides can be hired locally. Lake Taupo is the main centre for trout fishing, but numerous rivers and lakes on both islands are stocked with brown, rainbow and brook trout. Quinnat salmon can be caught in the rivers on the east coast of the South Island, the best months being January through to March.

New Zealand is also well known for its big-game fishing, particularly around the east coast of the North Island where marlin, broadbill, shark, yellowfin tuna and other pelagic species abound. The main season runs from January to May. Surfcasting and boat fishing are also very popular.

**NZ Professional Fishing Guides Association**, PO Box 16, Motu, Gisborne (tel: 06 863 5822).

## GOLF

Golfers will find no shortage of places to play – with around 400 golf-courses, New Zealand has more per head of population than anywhere else in the world. Many of the courses are set in beautiful scenery and may even include hazards such as boiling mud pools or sheep! Golf is a year-round activity and visitors are welcome at most clubs.

**New Zealand Golf Association**, PO Box 11 842, Wellington (tel: 04 472 2967).

## HORSE-RIDING

There are numerous opportunities for horse-riding, with half-day, full-day or longer treks available for all abilities. Most stables will supply all gear if necessary. Many country lodges and farmsteads offer their guests horse-riding.

**New Zealand Equestrian Federation**, PO Box 6146, Wellington (tel: 04 801 6449, fax: 04 801 7701).

of lift passes, lessons, ski hire and so on means that one in 10 New Zealanders can ski. Heli-skiing is also very popular, since the cost of reaching virgin, high-altitude runs by helicopter is very reasonable.

There are around 25 ski fields altogether, with most lying along the Southern Alps. The biggest winter resort is Queenstown, where the nearby Coronet Peak and Remarkables ski fields, have a wide variety of runs, all with fabulous views of lakes and mountains. The Cardrona and Treble Cone ski fields, near Wanaka, also offer a variety of terrain suitable for all skiers, from beginners to the advanced. Mount Hutt, inland from Christchurch, has the longest season in the country (late May to early November); other fields near by include Porter Heights, Dobson, Ohau and the country's newest ski area, Mount Lyford. On the North Island, the two main ski fields are Whakapapa and Turoa, both situated on the volcanic slopes of Mt Ruapehu (Tongariro National Park). For more information, see *The Official New Zealand Ski Guide*, published by the Tourism Board.

## HUNTING

Whereas it might be frowned upon elsewhere, recreational hunting is considered an important method of controlling the damage to native forests caused by New Zealand's large mammals. A permit is required to hunt in national parks. Some of the world's best deer-stalking is found in New Zealand, with autumn (March to May) being the optimum season. Chamois, thar, goats, pigs, opossums, rabbits, hares and wallabies can also be hunted.
**New Zealand Hunting and Fishing**, 210–212 Lake Terrace, Taupo (tel: 07 487 070, fax: 07 487 216).
**Conservation Department of Hunting Permits, Hut Passes, Walking Tracks and Camps**, Freephone 0800 268 600.

## SKIING

New Zealand is justifiably proud of its skiing facilities, and the relatively low cost

## WATER SPORTS

With its numerous lakes and rivers and over 10,000km of coastline, New Zealand has almost unparalleled opportunities for virtually every kind of water sport. Apart from rafting and jet-boating (see pages 146–50), canoeing and kayaking are also very popular, particularly sea kayaking in the sheltered waters of the Bay of Islands, the Marlborough Sounds and along the coast of the Abel Tasman National Park. One of the most popular canoeing rivers is the Whanganui, which has both rapids and long stretches of calm water. Rentals and/or organised tours are available in all these locations.

Surfing is possible all year round. In the

Lakes and harbours present numerous opportunities for messing about in boats

North Island, the most frequented beaches are those in the Auckland area, Raglan (west of Hamilton), around New Plymouth, Gisborne and Mount Manganui in the Bay of Plenty. In the South Island, beaches near Dunedin, Kaikoura and Westport are popular.

Scuba diving takes place mostly off the North Island where the sea is warmer; the top location is the Poor Knights Marine Reserve, offshore from Whangarei, which supports a wide variety of marine life. Other good spots include the Bay of Islands Maritime Park (which includes the wreck of the Greenpeace ship *Rainbow Warrior*, re-sunk here after it was destroyed by the French secret service in Auckland Harbour), Marlborough Sounds, the Hauraki Gulf, Stewart Island and even Fiordland.

## YACHTING

Yachting seems to be in the lifeblood of many New Zealanders, and charter boats of all kinds are available to visitors. Classic sailing areas include the Hauraki Gulf, Bay of Islands, Marlborough Sounds and the Coromandel Peninsula.

Given the Kiwi love of sailing, it is hardly surprising that they are enthusiastic followers of the America's Cup series, and the 1999–2000 challenge, which is being staged in Auckland, is eagerly awaited. Team New Zealand will defend their title against 18 challengers from around the world.

**New Zealand Canoeing Association**, PO Box 284, Wellington (tel: 04 472 3906).
**New Zealand Underwater Association**, PO Box 875, Auckland (tel: 09 849 5896).
**Yachting New Zealand**, PO Box 90–900, Auckland (tel: 09 303 2360).

Canoeing and kayaking are popular with both locals and visitors alike

# Food and Drink

*I*t has become something of a cliché to say that New Zealand has witnessed a 'culinary revolution' in recent years, but none the less this is true. You might still find plenty of stodgy food, meat pies and overdone steaks, but there are also hundreds of restaurants, wine bars and hotels where you can eat the best local produce cooked with imagination and flair.

## NATURAL INGREDIENTS

The raw ingredients have always been here, and it was only a matter of time before Kiwi chefs developed their own distinctive cuisine. The rich pasturelands and mild climate produce excellent beef and lamb, and deer are now also farmed extensively (local venison appears on menus as 'cervana', and has a much milder, less gamey taste than wild venison). Dairy products such as butter, cheese, milk, yoghurt and cream have always been of top quality.

New Zealanders are particularly partial to what the Maori call *kai-moana* (meaning 'food from the sea'), and some of the best eating fish include blue cod, snapper, orange roughy, John Dory, tarakihi, and hapuka (grouper). Shellfish are plentiful, and include rock lobsters (known as crayfish), scallops, Bluff

A *hangi*, or traditional Maori feast, should be tasted at least once

oysters and green-lipped mussels. Whitebait is a much-prized delicacy, usually served in fritters or sandwiches. You will also find salmon on the menu, but never trout, as it is illegal to buy or sell it.

Fresh fruit and vegetables grow in abundance, and apart from the usual standards such as apples, apricots, cherries, grapes, peaches, pears, nectarines, raspberries and strawberries, you should also try boysenberries, feijoa and tamarillos – not forgetting, of course, the ubiquitous kiwifruit.

The kiwifruit is just one of numerous succulent fruits which thrive in New Zealand soil

For the sweet-toothed, New Zealand has excellent ice-creams, flans and pastries, as well as the national dessert of pavlova, a rich concoction of meringue, whipped cream and fresh fruit.

## EATING PLACES

Almost every town and village has at least one tea shop serving refreshments and snacks. If you are in the middle of nowhere, the worst you can expect are plain meat pies and dry, lifeless sandwiches, but elsewhere pies, scones, pastries and sandwiches are often fresh, home-made and quite delicious.

Take-aways all over the country churn out fish and chips, pies and the like, often highly variable in quality. Pub food follows more or less the same format, although in cities and tourist areas some pubs have evolved into far more trendy places where you can get a decent meal in civilised surroundings.

Restaurants are either fully licensed (selling wines and spirits), licensed (wine and beer only) or BYO (bring your own alcohol, in which case a small corkage charge is added to the bill); some are both licensed and BYO. Wine bars and licensed cafés have also proliferated in recent years, and you will find plenty of places where you can enjoy a meal and a drink outdoors at pavement tables, Mediterranean-style.

Ethnic cuisine has had its impact and although Chinese take-ways predominate, there are also Greek, Italian, Mexican, Thai and Indian restaurants. Vegetarian food is widely available and usually very good.

## MAORI FEASTS

You should try a Maori *hangi* at least once. This is a feast of meat, seafood and vegetables (including the delicious *kumara*, or sweet potato, a Maori staple) steamed on heated stones in an 'earthen oven' (the *hangi*). The best *hangi* are those that follow an authentic Maori concert, although some hotels offer their own versions.

## BEER AND WINE

Beer is practically the national drink, and New Zealand lagers such as Kiwi Lager and Steinlager have won many international awards. Lion and DB are the two main brands served in pubs, but recently there has been a proliferation of 'boutique' or 'micro' breweries that produce excellent beers in small quantities. New Zealand wines have recently begun gaining international renown (see page 168).

# New Zealand Wineries

*T*he first vines were planted by the British Resident, James Busby, in his back garden at Waitangi in the 1840s, but it has only been during the last decade that the New Zealand wine industry has come of age.

### WINE TRAILS

In the major wine-growing areas, local tourist offices provide 'Wine Trail' brochures detailing the locations and opening hours of vineyards you can visit to taste and buy wines.

New Zealand wines are now exported worldwide

of Sauvignon comes from the Marlborough region.

The Chardonnay grape has also done very well here, producing a subtle, full-bodied wine. Gisborne is one of the prime Chardonnay areas, and the local wine-growers have many medals to their credit. Other successful white varieties are Gewürztraminer, Riesling and Müller-Thurgau.

### White wines

New Zealand's relatively cool climate is well adapted to vine-growing, with the long autumn giving the grapes a chance to ripen slowly, concentrating their flavour to the full. These conditions are ideally suited to Sauvignon Blanc, the slightly tart, 'grassy' grape which originates in France's Loire Valley. Nearly 60 per cent

### Red wines

Although New Zealand is well known for its white wines, progress has been slower with the reds. However, Cabernet Sauvignon seems to have found a natural home in the Hawke's Bay area and Pinot Noir, a notoriously fickle variety, is also doing well in the Martinborough district north of Wellington.

# Where to Eat

In these listings, the following symbols have been used to indicate the average cost of a meal per person, not including drinks:

**$** – up to NZ$15
**$$** – NZ$15–25
**$$$** – Over NZ$25

## NORTH ISLAND
### AUCKLAND
**Cin-Cin on the Quay $$$**
Busy brasserie on the quayside; extensive menu including New Zealand and Pacific dishes cooked with flair and imagination. Generous portions, efficient service. Reservations advised.
*Auckland Ferry Building, 99 Quay Street. Tel: 09 307 6966.*

**The Loaded Hog $–$$**
Cavernous bar and restaurant with good selection of snacks and main meals, all freshly prepared. The own-brand beers come from a micro-brewery visible through glass screens at the back.
*Viaduct Quay, corner of Hobson and Quay*

*streets. Tel: 09 3666 6491. Other branches in Wellington, Christchurch and Timaru.*

**Manifesto $–$$**
Trendy, atmospheric wine bar with good-value snacks and pasta meals.
*315 Queen Street. Tel: 09 303 4405.*

**Tony's $$–$$$**
Popular steakhouse with a wide selection of perfectly cooked cuts. Also lunches and other meals available.
*32 Lorne Street. Tel: 09 373 2138.*

### PAIHIA
**Kelly Tarlton's Tui $$**
Unusual café-restaurant on the barque *Tui* (see page 44). Good food, welcoming and informal. Licensed.
*By the bridge. Tel: 09 402 7018.*

**Tides $$**
Homely bistro specialising in venison, plus mussels, fresh fish and lamb dishes.
*Williams Road. Tel: 09 402 7557.*

### LAKE TAUPO
**The Bach $–$$**
Café–wine bar. Comfortable surroundings and good food complemented by an extensive wine list.
*Corner of Lake Terrace and Pataka Road. Tel: 07 378 7856.*

**Finch's Bar & Brasserie $$$**
Classic 'new wave' Kiwi cuisine prepared by an award-winning chef. Licensed.
*64 Tuwharetoa Street. Tel: 07 377 2425.*

**The Prawn Works $$$**
Prawns from the restaurant's own ponds feature in every conceivable combination. Bookings essential. Licensed. 20+.
*Prawn Park. Tel: 07 374 8303.*

Cin-Cin on the Quay, popular with the Auckland smart set

## ROTORUA
**Café Alzac $$**
Californian-style cuisine where you can
'graze' on speciality breads (focaccia,
bruschetta and the like) and a host of
unusual dishes including mussel and dill
chowder, pumpkin and herb gnocchi,
lamb fillet with black pudding salad, and
even kangaroo.
*59–61 Arawa Street. Tel: 07 347 2127.*
**Chez Bleu $$**
Café and bar. Casual dining offering
varied menu as well as Chez Bleu's own
'gourmet burgers'.
*160 Fenton Street. Tel: 07 348 1828.*
**Cobb & Co $$**
Busy, family-style restaurant (part of a
chain with establishments throughout
New Zealand and Australia) serving
steaks, seafood, 'roast of the day', chicken
dishes, and fish and chips. Specialities
include double ice-cream pies for dessert.
Reasonable value.
*Hinemoa Street. Tel: 07 348 2089.*
**Mr India $$**
Delicious tandoori cuisine, coupled with
good service.
*45 Amohau Street. Tel: 07 349 4940.*
**Roundabout Bar & Café $**
Lively, informal café-bar with a good
range of bar snacks, soups, salads, steaks,
burgers and vegetarian dishes. Generous
portions, excellent value.
*83 Arawa Street. Tel: 07 347 2553.*
**Sirocco Bar Café $–$$**
Cosy eating-house with a trendy,
Mediterranean-style atmosphere. Serves a
variety of bar snacks (nachos, sandwiches,
soups) and main-course pasta, seafood
and salads. Delicious desserts and good
coffee. Licensed. Good value.
*86 Eruera Street. Tel: 07 347 3388.*
**Zanelli's Italian Café & Restaurant $$**
Unpretentious, no-frills Italian restaurant
where the emphasis is on well-cooked,

well-presented classic dishes.
*23 Amohia Street. Tel: 07 348 4908.*

## WELLINGTON
**Aroma Café-Bar $**
Fresh-cooked, home-made pasta in a
variety of sauces, as well as other Italian
favourites, home-made breads and
excellent coffee make this self-service
cafeteria a popular spot.
*Dukes Arcade, corner of Willis and Manners
streets. Tel: 04 499 1154.*
**The Backbench Party $$–$$$**
Light and airy pub opposite Parliament
with a jovial atmosphere (plenty of
political cartoons and so on). A fun
theme pub.
*Corner of Kate Shepherd Place and
Molesworth Street. Tel: 04 472 3065.*
**The Malthouse $$**
Spacious bar in the heart of the city with
a terrace and conservatory. The
adjoining carvery has five different roasts
on offer daily, plus a blackboard menu.
Good food, reasonable prices.
*Willis Street. Tel: 04 499 4355.*

# SOUTH ISLAND
## CHRISTCHURCH
**Canterbury Tales $$$**
Located in the city's top hotel, this
elegant restaurant (with tapestries
depicting Chaucerian scenes on the
walls) has an extensive menu and is
deservedly popular. Bookings essential.
*Parkroyal Hotel. Tel: 03 365 7799.*
**Gloucester Street Café & Bar $–$$**
Good value for light meals, with
reasonably priced daily blackboard
specials and imaginative vegetarian
dishes. Licensed.
*96 Gloucester Street. Tel: 03 379 8298.*
**Mainstreet Café & Bar $–$$**
Rated as one of the best vegetarian
restaurants in New Zealand, with tasty

and imaginative food at reasonable prices. Licensed and BYO.
*Corner of Colombo and Salisbury streets. Tel: 03 365 0421.*

### Oxford on Avon $–$$
Good value meals are the order of the day in this pub-restaurant situated beside the River Avon.
*794 Colombo Street. Tel: 03 379 7148.*

### Willowbank $$–$$$
This excellent licensed restaurant is part of a wildlife reserve (see page 109), and you can view the wildlife at night after eating. Guided tours are free to diners, and offer the chance to see kiwis and other nocturnal species in their natural (floodlit) bush habitat.
*Willowbank Wildlife Reserve, Hussey Road. Tel: 03 359 6226.*

## DUNEDIN
### High Tide $–$$
Quiet waterside restaurant that serves meat and seafood dishes..
*29 Kitchener Street. Tel: 03 477 9784.*

### Homestead Restaurant $$–$$$
This restaurant is situated amidst magnificent woodlands at, 'the hidden valley' of Glenfalloch. Fine cuisine; BYO and licensed.
*430 Portobello Road. Tel: 03 476 1006. Ten minutes from the city centre.*

### Lone Star $–$$
Lively atmosphere, part of a highly popular chain of Tex-Mex restaurants. Licensed.
*417 Princes Street. Tel: 03 474 1955. Other branches in Christchurch and Queenstown.*

## QUEENSTOWN
### Avanti $
Better than average selection of pizzas, soups and Italian dishes is on offer in this cheerful and reasonably cheap

One of the excellent restaurants in Christchurch

restaurant. No reservations; BYO.
*20 The Mall. Tel: 03 442 8503.*

### The Cow $–$$
Very cosy and popular pizza and spaghetti house in an old stone building, with a roaring fire. Book in advance or expect a long wait.
*Cow Lane. Tel: 03 442 8588.*

### Fishbone Bar & Grill $$–$$$
Good seafood and fish dishes in an unpretentious, café-style setting. Oysters, mussels, calamari, crayfish, fish fillets and so on are served in generous portions, so go with a hearty appetite if you want more than one course.
Licensed and BYO.
*Beach Street. Tel: 03 442 6768.*

### Stonewall Café $$
Fish, pasta and fresh seasonal dishes prepared in simple but imaginative ways. Classic, tempting desserts.
*The Mall. Tel: 03 442 6429.*

# Hotels and Accommodation

New Zealand has a huge range of accommodation to suit every budget, ranging from campsites in national parks to stylish country retreats and smart city business hotels. There is rarely a problem, even in the most remote location, of finding a clean, comfortable room, although during the peak summer season (mid-December to January) you may need to telephone ahead to make reservations in popular tourist centres such as Rotorua and Queenstown. Advance reservations are also necessary for up-market country lodges and places with very limited accommodation options, such as the Mount Cook National Park.

One of the more useful publications, covering numerous options all over the country, is the *New Zealand Where to Stay Guide*, published by the tourism board in conjunction with the New Zealand Automobile Association (NZAA). A new system of classification

Moderately-priced motels are found in almost every corner of the country

for accommodation has been introduced under the 'Qualmark' logo; developed by the tourism board in conjunction with the New Zealand AA, hotels and all other lodgings will be graded with a one-to five-star rating system.

**Luxury hotels**

International chain hotels such as Sheraton, Regent and Hyatt are found in the major cities and resorts, alongside locally owned hotel chains such as the Pacific Park Group and Scenic Circle Hotels. Many of the prime tourist hotels in the country that were once part of the government-owned Tourist Hotel Corporation are now operated by Southern Pacific Hotels. The costs of a room in an international-standard hotel ranges from around NZ$200 to over NZ$1,000 a night for de luxe suites.

**Retreats and sporting lodges**

Wilderness hideaways are something of a New Zealand speciality, and if your budget allows it you should certainly try to stay in one of these exclusive, highly individual retreats for a few days. Exceptionally high standards of accommodation, coupled with good food, plenty of atmosphere and first-class facilities are the hallmarks of this type of lodge. Many concentrate on hunting and fishing, with professional guides on tap (the world-renowned Huka Lodge and Tongariro Lodge, both near Lake Taupo, are sports-oriented), while others are remarkable for their beautiful natural surroundings – such as the excellent Puka Park Lodge in the Coromandel and Moose Lodge on Lake Rotoiti.

Around two dozen lodges are

Backpacker hostels catering for young travellers often have good facilities

described in the booklet *The Lodges of New Zealand*, which features exclusive resorts and sporting lodges, available from the tourism board.

**Motor inns, motels and other hotels**

Although there is quite a lot of overlap between these categories, motor inns usually have more facilities than motels, with a house bar, swimming-pool, licensed restaurant and so on. They include chains such as Flag Hotels, Best Western, Quality Inns, Autolodge and Manor Motor Inns. Expect to pay NZ$80–200 per night.

Motels are located everywhere and provide one of the best options for mid-market, independent travellers. The clean, comfortable units usually have one or more bedrooms, a lounge and a reasonably well-equipped kitchen. Some also have swimming-pools, spa pools, in-house video channels, laundry rooms and other facilities. You can often find motel rooms from NZ$50 in the off-season. Many motels are affiliated to booking

chains – for example, Jason's, Flag Hotels and Best Western.

New Zealand also has numerous independent hotels, often older buildings in town or city centres. Budget rooms in these hotels are invariably one of the cheapest options (apart from hostels or backpacker accommodation), costing from around NZ$20–30. However, standards vary widely and at these prices your room is unlikely to have a private bathroom. Some historic hotels (such as the Brian Boru in Thames) have been renovated to higher standards and still represent good value for money.

Around 50 historic hotels and country pubs are listed in the *Pub Beds Guide* (available from Pub Beds, PO Box 32–332, Auckland; tel: 09 443 0888; enclose SAE).

Accommodation throughout the country is covered in the AA Accommodation Guide *Jason's Motels and Motor Lodges* (NZ$9.95 from bookshops or free when you stay in a listed property).

are high-country sheep stations; these have purpose-built facilities where you can stay in complete luxury and take part in almost anything you want, from hunting expeditions to heli-sking. Some (such as the Mount Hutt Station Resort) even have international-standard restaurants and conference facilities!

You can arrange accommodation at farmstays for just one night or for a whole holiday, and your room may either be in the family home or in a separate unit or farm cottage. Rates start as low as NZ$20–30 for shared, self-catering units, reaching around NZ$70–80 for full board and rooms with private facilities. There are several agencies which specialise in bookings:

**Rural Holidays New Zealand Ltd**, PO Box 2155, Christchurch (tel: 03 366 1919; fax: 03 379 3087).
**New Zealand Farm Holidays Ltd**, PO Box 256, Silverdale, Auckland (tel: 09 426 5430; fax: 09 426 8474).
**New Zealand Home Hospitality**, PO Box 309, Nelson (tel: 03 548 2424; fax: 03 546 9519).

## Guest-houses and bed and breakfast accommodation

Staying in a private guest-house or B&B is a good way to meet people and find out about the locality. Again, standards vary widely: a room in a basic guest-house costs from NZ$30 per person, while one in a more comfortable B&B establishment where breakfast (usually huge!) is included will set you back around NZ$40–60, per person. The *New Zealand Bed & Breakfast Book* by J and J Thomas (Moonshine Press, Wellington) is a good source of information.

## Farmstays and homestays

The difference between farmstays and B&Bs is that at the former you usually get the chance to take part in day-to-day activities and learn about the Kiwi way of life; you will be staying in a real family home and will usually share home-cooked meals with your hosts. On farmstays you can help out with activities such as shearing and milking, and a range of other outdoor activities (bush-walking, fishing, cycling and so on) is usually available. Homestays are an urban version of the farmstay.

An up-market variation on farmstays

## Hostels and backpacker accommodation

Hostels are as common in New Zealand as motels, providing clean, basic accommodation almost everywhere tourists are likely to go – and a few more places besides. Whilst there are numerous 'official' hostels (run by the YHA, YMCA and YWCA), there are also hundreds more private hostels – usually called 'backpackers'.

Gone are the days of segregated dormitories and lights out by 10pm: hostels now have private rooms as well as a more liberal attitude. Communal facilities usually include kitchens, lounge areas, laundries and so on, and although you may sometimes have to provide your own bedding this can often be hired for a small charge. Nightly costs are around NZ$12–20.

Numerous sources of information, including *New Zealand Budget Backpackers Accommodation*, *Backpackers Guide to New Zealand* and the *New Zealand Backpackers Hotels* information booklet are available from information centres and hostels.

### Camping and motorcamps

There are well equipped campsites all over the country. Some also have cabins and/or 'tourist flats' attached. Campsite costs start at around NZ$8 per adult, while powered sites for motorhomes are around NZ$9–10 per adult. The Camp and Cabin Association (CCA) produces a leaflet, *Holiday Accommodation Parks*, which gives details on sites operated by its members, who have to meet certain minimum standards. The leaflet is available from the CCA, PO Box 394, Paraparaumu. The AA Accommodation Guide also provides detailed listings of motor camps and caravan parks.

The Department of Conservation (DOC) maintains a network of huts and campsites in national parks and other wilderness areas. Facilities range from the basic minimum to fully serviced campgrounds with hot showers, laundry facilities, lighting and so on. Costs are minimal (NZ$2–9). Locations and facilities are given in *Conservation Campsites*, available at DOC information centres or from the DOC, PO Box 10420, Wellington.

### Thomas Cook Traveller's Tip

Travellers who purchase their travel tickets from a Thomas Cook network location are entitled to use the services of any other Thomas Cook network location, free of charge, to make hotel reservations (see list on page 185).

A campervan will give you the flexibility of your own home on wheels

# On Business

$S$ince the mid-1980s, the New Zealand economy has undergone a programme of wide-ranging reforms designed to create an open, more competitive business environment. During the 1980s growth remained sluggish as successive governments pushed through these structural reforms, but the benefits are now beginning to filter through and, aside from a short recession in 1990 and 1991, the economy has been growing at a rate of just over 7 per cent per annum, with inflation lying below 2 per cent.

## BUSINESS AND INVESTMENT ENVIRONMENT

Foreign investors are welcomed in New Zealand, particularly in sectors contributing to foreign-exchange earnings such as tourism and the export of locally manufactured processed goods. Businesses are now subject to much less regulation than they used to be, and the transfer of funds in and out of the country is not restricted. The sale of major national assets to foreign investors has been encouraged, and similar policies are still being pursued; there are no ceilings on the level of non-resident ownership of privatised state enterprises.

Incentives are sometimes available to foreign investors, and investment is widely promoted through bodies such as the Tourist Development Board and the New Zealand Import Export Corporation. Foreign investment is monitored and controlled by the Overseas Investment Commission (OIC), but consent is not required for investments below a value threshold of NZ$10 million – unless they are related to broadcasting, commercial fishing or rural land. Stock exchanges operate in Auckland, Wellington, Christchurch and Dunedin.

## BUSINESS ETIQUETTE

New Zealand's business culture lies somewhere between that of Britain and the United States, with a fast-growing entrepreneurial sector which has a highly positive outlook on the economic future. Doing business in New Zealand is the same as doing business in any other advanced nation, and you will generally find the people are helpful, efficient and straightforward in their dealings.

## BUSINESS HOURS

Offices and businesses operate Monday to Friday, 8.30am–5pm. Trading banks open Monday to Friday, 9.30am–4.30pm.

## COMMUNICATIONS

See **Post Offices** on page 186 and **Telephones** on pages 188–9. Fax machines are widely used, and conference calls and satellite links can easily be arranged. Pagers and cellular telephones can be hired.

## CONFERENCES

The largest conference centres are the Auckland Convention Centre, Christchurch Town Hall, the Wellington Festival and Convention Centre, the new Rotorua Convention and Exhibition Centre, the Trafalgar Centre in Nelson and the Dunedin Centre, all of which have single room capacities of over 2,000 people. Hotels such as the Carlton,

Wellington is New Zealand's business capital

Sheraton and Hyatt in Auckland have facilities for over 1,000 people, and there are numerous other venues around the country capable of accommodating anything from 10 to 500 people. Professional Conference Organisers (PCOs) are available to help plan and manage conventions on any scale.

Further details from: **The New Zealand Convention Association**, PO Box 331202, Takapuna, Auckland (tel: 09 4864 128; fax: 09 4864 126).

## SECRETARIAL SERVICES

A full range of secretarial and business services is available in the main cities, where you will also find short- or long-term serviced office space to rent. Hotels catering specifically for executive travellers, such as the Regent in Auckland, have business centres with all the usual facilities.

## FURTHER INFORMATION

The international accountancy firm of Ernst & Young produces the book *Doing Business in New Zealand*, which details taxation laws, company structures, financial reporting and the like. It is available from the company's overseas branches or from:

**Ernst & Young, National Mutual Centre**, 37–41 Shortland Street, Auckland (tel: 09 377 4790; fax: 09 309 8137).

Another useful address is:

**Ministry of Foreign Affairs and Trade**, 38–40 The Terrace, Private Bag, Wellington (tel: 04 472 8877; fax: 04 472 9596).

# Practical Guide

**CONTENTS**
Arriving
Camping
Children
Climate
Conversion Tables
Crime
Electricity
Embassies and Consulates
Emergency Telephone Numbers
Getting Around
Health
Insurance
Lost Property
Media
Money Matters
Opening Hours
Pharmacies
Places of Worship
Police
Post
Public and School Holidays
Public Transport
Senior Citizens
Student and Youth Travel
Telephones
Time
Tipping
Toilets
Tourist Offices
Travellers with Disabilities

## ARRIVING

### By air

Auckland is the main international gateway for passengers arriving in New Zealand, although increasing numbers of airlines are also flying into Christchurch in the South Island. Because of limited runway capacity, Wellington only handles flights to and from Australia. Air New Zealand, the national carrier, has flights to Australia, Japan, Singapore, Malaysia, Hong Kong, Taiwan, the USA and Europe, either directly or via the Pacific Islands. Over 20 other international airlines operate scheduled services to New Zealand.

Auckland's international terminal has all the usual banking and exchange facilities, luggage storage, and visitor information centres for accommodation reservations, sightseeing and onward travel arrangements. Special elevators and toilet facilities are available for the disabled. Auckland airport (AKL) lies 22km from the city centre, and taxis are fairly expensive (around NZ$40). At least three companies operate shuttle buses (costing NZ$9 one way) which pick up at both the domestic and international terminals and drop off at any city-centre hotel or other location. Christchurch (10km northwest) and Wellington (8km southeast) airports have similar facilities.

An airport departure tax of NZ$20 is payable by all passengers leaving on international flights.

### By sea

There are no regular passenger services but some round-the-world cruises call in at New Zealand. Arriving by yacht is a distinct possibility, since many cruising yachts take on casual crews at various points in the South Pacific before visiting New Zealand.

### Customs

There are no exchange controls or restrictions on the import or export of

currency. Aside from personal effects,
visitors are allowed to bring in 200
cigarettes, 250g tobacco or 50 cigars, one
bottle of spirits and 4.5 litres of wine.

New Zealand has remained largely
free of most plant and animal diseases
and there are strict controls on the import
of foodstuffs and plant and animal
material. Aircraft cabins are sprayed with
an insecticide before passengers leave the
aircraft, to ensure no unwanted insects
are carried off, and if you are carrying
walking boots, these may be confiscated,
but returned to you cleaned!

If you are planning to go fishing you
may bring your own rods, but lures or
flies containing feathers will need to be
fumigated. Hunters should check
firearms regulations with their nearest
embassy before departure (see page
182), but in general, hunting rifles may
be brought in. A firearms permit is
compulsory, obtainable from the police
after a declaration to customs officers
upon arrival.

The import of narcotics is prohibited,
and sniffer dogs are used regularly in
arrival halls.

### Documents
No vaccination certificates are necessary.
Passports must be valid for at least three
months beyond your intended departure
date. Visitors may be granted entry for
up to three months, although this can be
extended for up to a year for genuine
tourists. Visitors must hold fully paid
onward or return tickets, and sufficient
funds to keep themselves whilst in the
country. Everybody has to complete an
arrival card. Visas are normally only
required for visitors intending to work or
study, or if you are being sponsored
during your visit by a friend, relative or
business organisation.

Campsites are often on the edge of
wilderness

### CAMPING
Camping may be permitted on any
suitable public open space (apart from
those designated 'No Camping') or on
private property subject to the owners'
permission. For details on campsites,
see page 175.

### CHILDREN
See pages 160–1.

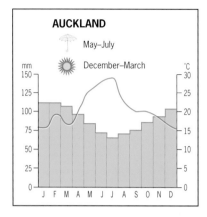

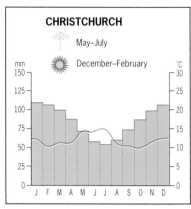

## CLIMATE

The seasons in New Zealand are the reverse of those in the northern hemisphere: summer runs from December to March, autumn from March to May, winter from June to August, and spring from September to November. However, seasonal variations are not extreme, and a mild winter can often lead to spring growths appearing at the end of July; conversely, autumn weather often carries over well into June in northerly latitudes.

Because the sun is in the northern sky, temperatures are highest in the far north (where summers are subtropical) and lowest in the far south (where winters are closer to subantarctic, but only for short periods). Average daily sunshine figures are seven to eight hours in summer, and four to five hours in winter. Most places get around 2,000 hours of sunshine a year, with the north of the North Island and the north of the South Island slightly above average with around 2,350 hours or more.

Rainfall is spread fairly evenly throughout the year, averaging 600–1,200mm. The prevailing winds are westerly, and the backbone of mountains which runs right through the country ensures that the western side therefore receives a much higher rainfall than eastern areas; this is particularly marked in the South Island, where the altitude of the Southern Alps means that rain falls on the western coast almost constantly. The highest rainfall is in Fiordland, and although it doesn't rain every day here it does tend to bucket it down. Snow falls on the mountains and hills (particularly in the South Island) during winter. Auckland and the far north have the hottest and most humid summers, while those around Marlborough and Nelson are comfortably hot and dry. The coldest winters and hottest summers are both found in central Otago. Wellington is exposed to southerly winds off the Cook Strait (which keep the temperature down all year), as well as occasional gales.

Although seasonal variations aren't dramatic, the weather is highly changeable and may alter several times during the course of the day in any one place, so be prepared for both rain and sun almost all year round. When the sun does shine (even behind cloud cover), it can burn very quickly (see page 28).

## CONVERSION TABLES

See tables opposite.

## CRIME

New Zealand has always had a reputation as a remarkably safe destination, and although it still doesn't have a high level of serious crime there have been noticeable increases in recent years in assault, rape and petty theft – sometimes involving tourists. Take the same commonsense precautions you would anywhere else: avoid dark city backstreets at night; don't leave cameras, videos or other valuables on view in parked cars; don't leave your car unlocked; make use of hotel safes if carrying large amounts of cash or valuables; and, finally, make sure you are fully insured for loss or damage.

## ELECTRICITY

The electricity supply is 230–240 volts/50 hertz. Hotels and motels provide 110-volt AC sockets for shavers only (rated at 20 watts). For all other equipment you will need an adaptor for flat, three- or two-pin plugs (these are readily available in major hardware stores), but check that your equipment can operate on 230–240 volts first.

### Conversion Table

| FROM | TO | MULTIPLY BY |
|------|------|------|
| Inches | Centimetres | 2.54 |
| Feet | Metres | 0.3048 |
| Yards | Metres | 0.9144 |
| Miles | Kilometres | 1.6090 |
| Acres | Hectares | 0.4047 |
| Gallons | Litres | 4.5460 |
| Ounces | Grams | 28.35 |
| Pounds | Grams | 453.6 |
| Pounds | Kilograms | 0.4536 |
| Tons | Tonnes | 1.0160 |

To convert back, for example from centimetres to inches, divide by the number in the third column.

### Men's Suits

| | | | | | | | |
|------|------|------|------|------|------|------|------|
| UK | 36 | 38 | 40 | 42 | 44 | 46 | 48 |
| Rest of Europe | 46 | 48 | 50 | 52 | 54 | 56 | 58 |
| US | 36 | 38 | 40 | 42 | 44 | 46 | 48 |

### Dress Sizes

| | | | | | | |
|------|------|------|------|------|------|------|
| UK | 8 | 10 | 12 | 14 | 16 | 18 |
| France | 36 | 38 | 40 | 42 | 44 | 46 |
| Italy | 38 | 40 | 42 | 44 | 46 | 48 |
| Rest of Europe | 34 | 36 | 38 | 40 | 42 | 44 |
| US | 6 | 8 | 10 | 12 | 14 | 16 |

### Men's Shirts

| | | | | | | | |
|------|------|------|------|------|------|------|------|
| UK | 14 | 14.5 | 15 | 15.5 | 16 | 16.5 | 17 |
| Rest of Europe | 36 | 37 | 38 39/40 | 41 | | 42 | 43 |
| US | 14 | 14.5 | 15 | 15.5 | 16 | 16.5 | 17 |

### Men's Shoes

| | | | | | | | |
|------|------|------|------|------|------|------|------|
| UK | 7 | 7.5 | 8.5 | | 9.5 | 10.5 | 11 |
| Rest of Europe | 41 | 42 | 43 | | 44 | 45 | 46 |
| US | 8 | 8.5 | 9.5 | | 10.5 | 11.5 | 12 |

### Women's Shoes

| | | | | | | | |
|------|------|------|------|------|------|------|------|
| UK | 4.5 | 5 | 5.5 | 6 | | 6.5 | 7 |
| Rest of Europe | 38 | 38 | 39 | 39 | | 40 | 41 |
| US | 6 | 6.5 | 7 | 7.5 | | 8 | 8.5 |

## EMBASSIES AND CONSULATES
### New Zealand Embassies Overseas
**Australia** New Zealand High Commission, Commonwealth Avenue, Canberra, ACT 2600 (tel: 612 627 04211).

**Canada** New Zealand High Commission, Metropolitan House, Suite 727, 99 Bank Street, Ottawa, Ontario KIP 6G3 (tel: 613 238 5991).

**UK** New Zealand High Commission, New Zealand House, 80 Haymarket, London SW1Y 4TQ (tel: 0171 930 8422).

**US** New Zealand Embassy, 37 Observatory Circle NW, Washington, DC20008 (tel: 1 202/328 4848). There are also consulates in Los Angeles and New York.

### Foreign representation in New Zealand:
**American Embassy** 29 Fitzherbert Terrace, Wellington (tel: 04 472 2068).
**Australian High Commission** 72 Hobson Street, Thorndon, Wellington (tel: 04 473 6411).
**British High Commission** 44 Hill Street, Thorndon, Wellington (tel: 04 472 6049).
**Canadian High Commission** ICI House, 61 Molesworth Street, Wellington (tel: 04 473 9577).
**Irish Consulate** 87 Queen Street, Auckland (tel: 09 302 2867).

## EMERGENCY TELEPHONE NUMBERS
Dial 111 and ask for police, fire or ambulance. Travellers who have bought their tickets at any Thomas Cook Network location can obtain free emergency assistance at any Thomas Cook Network office in New Zealand. Thomas Cook MasterCard travellers' cheque refund (tel: 0800 440112).

## GETTING AROUND
### By air
The major towns, cities and tourist destinations in New Zealand are served by flights on Air New Zealand, Ansett New Zealand and Mount Cook Airlines.

The three main airlines all offer travel passes for overseas visitors (with discounts on normal tickets), either for a set number of sectors or for a limited period of time (usually one month).

Air New Zealand's air pass has to be bought overseas before you travel to New Zealand, but both the Ansett and Mount Cook Airlines passes can be purchased after your arrival.

In addition, Air New Zealand offers Thrifty Fares (40 per cent discount; must be purchased overseas) and Off-Peak Saver fares (20 per cent discount; can be bought at the time of flying) on off-peak domestic flights.

### Domestic airlines
**Air New Zealand** (tel: 09 357 3000).
**Ansett New Zealand** (tel: 09 302 2146).
**Mount Cook Airlines** (tel: 09 309 5395).

**By rail**, see page 187.

### Car hire
All the big international agencies have rental depots in the major cities and tourist areas. You will need a current national or international driving licence; the minimum age for rentals is 21 years. Insurance is compulsory, and is usually included in hire charges.

Hire charges can be fairly expensive (standard high-season charges are around NZ$90 per day or NZ$80 per day for a one-week hire). If you plan to tour the whole of New Zealand by car you can often negotiate discounts with the companies direct.

A mural in MacKenzie Country, below the Southern Alps. Tourists are made to feel welcome

Campervans are another alternative for small groups or families, giving you a great deal of flexibility on accommodation and freedom to camp anywhere. Rates start from around NZ$144 per day in low season for a two-berth van, to NZ$228 per day for a four to six berth in high season. The main agency is Maui Tours.

**Avis**, 17/19 Nelson Street, Auckland (tel: 09 379 2650).

**Budget**, 83 Beach Road, Auckland (tel: 09 375 2230).

**Hertz**, 154 Victoria Street West, Auckland (tel: 09 309 0989).

**National Car Rental**, Princes Wharf, Auckland (tel: 09 309 3336).

UK-based travellers can obtain flexible packages from Thomas Cook Holidays which include car rental, rail pass and accommodation options, or even fully inclusive tours, at advantageous rates (details from any branch of Thomas Cook).

### Driving

New Zealand has an excellent, well-signposted road network and (apart from urban areas) traffic is generally light. Driving is on the left; speed limits are generally 100kph on motorways and the open road and 50kph in built-up areas, but other limits may be indicated.

In backcountry areas and forests the roads are often unsealed, these being known variously as gravel roads or unmetalled roads.

Restrictions may apply in some areas if you have a rental car, although these are usually ignored (there's not much point in hiring a car here if you can't take it to some of the most unspoiled wilderness areas!).

Take extra care driving on unsealed roads, and watch out for the large grading machines. Heavy rains may also cause road slumps, which leave holes on the edge of the road.

### Breakdowns

Many rental companies will include free breakdown services as part of the package. Members of the Automobile Association are offered free reciprocal membership of the AA in New Zealand, including breakdown assistance, the provision of maps, touring advice and accommodation guides.

In the South Island in particular, it is always a good idea to fill up with petrol as the next service station may be some distance away. If you do run out (or even think you are about to run out), rural cafés and shops usually have emergency petrol for sale in small quantities.

### Hitch-hiking

Hitch-hiking is perfectly acceptable (and legal) in New Zealand, and although it is far safer here than in many other countries you should still exercise common sense and reasonable care in accepting lifts. Women should not hitch-hike alone.

### HEALTH

New Zealand is a clean, healthy country and tap water is safe to drink everywhere. However, the parasite *giardia* has been found in some lakes, rivers and streams, and can cause diarrhoea if it gets into your system. The probability of catching *giardia* is fairly remote, but if you are camping it is best either to boil water for three minutes and then add iodine solution or chlorine bleach, or use a *giardia*-rated water filter.

Public and private health-care facilities operate to high standards, and in case of illness your hotel or motel will be able to arrange a local doctor (otherwise, see 'Doctors and Medical Services' at the front of telephone directories).

If you have an accident you will be covered by the Accident Compensation Scheme and entitled to make a claim to the Accident Compensation Corporation, irrespective of blame. Allowable benefits include some medical and hospital expenses and compensation for permanent disability – but not for loss of earnings outside the country. The existence of this scheme means that it is not possible to sue for damages in the courts for accidental injury or death. Like every other part of the world, AIDS is present.

### INSURANCE

A comprehensive personal travel-insurance policy is highly advisable. Despite the Accident Compensation Scheme (see above), make sure your policy covers personal accidents as not all costs will be covered. Cover for loss of personal possessions and travel delay is also recommended. Note that most policies automatically exclude adventure sports such as white-water rafting and skiing, so if you are planning to take part in these activities you might want to arrange for an extension to the cover. Contact a specialist travel insurance company who will normally provide cover for most sporting activities considered 'dangerous', except bungee jumping.

### LOST PROPERTY

Always inform the police as soon as possible if you lose any valuables. If you need to make an insurance claim for valuable items, remember you will need to obtain a copy of your statement from the police. Lost credit cards or travellers' cheques should always be reported within 24 hours to the issuing company.

## MEDIA
### Television and radio
There are four main television channels: Television One (current affairs and sport); Television Two (light entertainment); and TV3 and Channel 4 show a variety of programmes. All channels carry commercials. Sky TV is also available (including CNN News) in hotels and motels. Also VHF channels broadcasting in many areas with various topic channels.

There are many FM radio stations; also two non-commercial stations: the AM National Programme (mainly news, documentaries, drama and the like); and the FM Concert Programme (classical music).

Tourist FM Radio (in English on 88.2MHz) provides visitors with 24-hour information on history and culture, local activities and attractions.

### Newspapers and magazines
There is no national newspaper as such, although the *New Zealand Herald* (published in Auckland) has the highest daily circulation, closely followed by the *Dominion* (published in Wellington). In addition, there are another 30 or so morning and evening dailies, plus three national Sunday newspapers. Tourist newspapers are also produced in resort areas.

International magazines are widely available. The best local magazine is Auckland's *Metro*, published monthly. The fortnightly *Te Maori News* is mostly written in English. One of the best current affairs magazines is the monthly *North and South*.

## MONEY MATTERS
The New Zealand dollar (NZ$) is divided into 100 cents, with notes in denominations of $5, $10, $20, $50 and $100, and coins of 5, 10, 20, 50 cents, $1 and $2.

Banks are open Monday to Friday, 9.30am–4.30pm, except public holidays. Bureaux de change, which can be found in most major resorts, are open longer hours and often at weekends. Automated teller machines (ATMs) are widespread and can be used with international PIN numbers to obtain cash.

Travellers' cheques can be changed in banks, hotels, and in large stores in cities and in tourist areas. All international credit cards (American Express, Diners Club, JCB, Visa and MasterCard) are widely accepted.

Thomas Cook branches throughout New Zealand can change all major currencies and will cash Thomas Cook travellers' cheques free of commission, as well as providing emergency assistance in cases of loss or theft. They can be found in the following places of tourist interest: 34 Queen Street, Auckland (tel: 09 377 2666); corner of Hinemo and Fenton streets, Rotorua (tel: 07 347 0111); corner of Armagh and Colombo streets, Christchurch; 358 Lambton Quay, Wellington.

The last two are full travel shops and will also provide services such as car rental and other travel arrangements.

## OPENING HOURS
Shops are usually open Monday to Friday, 9am–5.30pm, with late-night shopping until 8.30 or 9pm one or two nights a week (usually Thursday or Friday). Some shops close at 12.30 or 1pm on Saturdays (4.30pm in larger centres), while others stay open all day. Many tourist shops and some travel agents are open longer hours. Many supermarkets, grocery stores and some

retail chains are also open on Sunday. Local food shops (known as dairies) are usually open seven days a week, 7am–10pm. Petrol (gas) stations are also open longer hours (many are open 24 hours), and stock food and other sundries.

## PHARMACIES

Known by the English term 'Chemists', pharmacies are open during normal shopping hours and most cities also have urgent dispensaries that open outside these hours (listed under 'Hospitals' in the front of telephone directories). Pharmacies also stock a wide range of other products such as sun-block, cosmetics, photographic film and so on.

## PLACES OF WORSHIP

The major Christian denominations are Anglican, Presbyterian, Methodist, Baptist and Roman Catholic, each with places of worship in most towns and cities. There are also synagogues and mosques in the larger cities. Your hotel reception will be able to advise on the times of services.

## POLICE

Dial 111 for the police, fire and ambulance.

## POST

Post shops are open Monday to Friday, 9am–5pm, and stamps can also be bought in grocery shops, bookshops and stationers. The two main types of postal service are standard post (which delivers the next day across town and in two to three working days nationwide) and fast post (international mail, plus next-day delivery between major towns and cities within the country). A poste restante service is available at many branches.

## PUBLIC AND SCHOOL HOLIDAYS

Most businesses and all banks are closed on public holidays; all shops are closed on Christmas Day and Good Friday except for a few convenience stores and petrol stations.

**1 and 2 January** New Year
**6 February** Waitangi Day
**March/April** Good Friday and Easter Monday
**25 April** Anzac Day
**First Monday in June** Queen's Birthday
**Fourth Monday in October** Labour Day
**25 December** Christmas Day
**26 December** Boxing Day

There are also regional holidays which correspond to the founding days of each of the country's 13 provinces.

During school holidays you are strongly advised to book ahead for accommodation in the more popular holiday resorts.

**Summer** mid-December to the beginning of February
**April** middle two weeks
**Mid-term** early July
**September/October** late September/early October 2 weeks.

## PUBLIC TRANSPORT
### Coaches

The InterCity network, Newmans Coaches, Mount Cook Landlines and Magic Bus services between them connect most towns and cities in the country. All the operators offer coach passes, either with discounts on various sectors or for periods ranging from seven to 35 days. Several companies offer backpackers 'alternative' coach services, either within a particular region or across the whole country, which stop off at places of interest. You can hop off some of these services and rejoin the next one that comes along if you want to stay somewhere longer. One of the better known companies offering these services is Kiwi Experience, which has five different routes all over the country.

**InterCity Travel Centre**, Railway Station, Beach Road, Auckland (tel: 09 639 0500).
**Kiwi Experience**, 36 Customs Street, Auckland (tel: 09 366 9830).
**Mount Cook Landlines**, Queen Street, Auckland tel: (toll-free) 0800 800 287).
**Magic Bus**, PO Box 945, Union House, 36–8 Quay Street, Auckland (tel: 09 358 5600).
**Newmans Coaches**, PO Box 90-821, Auckland (tel: 09 309 9738).

### Ferries

The main form of transport between the North and South Islands is the Inter-Island ferry, which operates between Wellington and Picton three or four times daily, with a crossing time of just over three hours. The ferry offers a roll-on, roll-off service for cars, and although passenger bookings are rarely necessary, cars should be pre-booked in peak periods (December to February and on public holidays). Make bookings through any travel agent, railway station or tel: (toll-free) 0800 658 999.

### Rail

New Zealand Rail operates daily services between Auckland and Wellington, Auckland and Rotorua and Taurango, and Wellington and Napier in the North Island, and between Christchurch and Picton, Invercargill and the TranzAlpine to the West Coast at Greymouth, and other west coast towns on the South Island. There are four different price bands for rail tickets: Standard, Economy, Saver and Super Saver, the last three of

Watch out for single-lane bridges, which are found even on the main highways

which offer various discount levels if tickets are purchased in advance (within the country).
**New Zealand Rail**, Private Bag, Wellington. Central reservations, tel: (toll-free) 0800 802 802 or 09 498 3000 from outside New Zealand.

### New Zealand Travelpass

As well as the individual travel passes that are available for air, rail and coach travel, you can also buy a combined travel pass for trains, coaches and ferries (a 3-in-1 Travelpass) or one which also includes an air travel sector on Ansett NZ (a 4-in-1 Travelpass). The variations of packages for the 3-in-1 and 4-in-1 Travel Passes range from 5 days travel over 10 days, to 22 days travel over 8 weeks. these passes can be bought outside New Zealand or on arrival. Contact Travelpass New Zealand, PO Box 785, Auckland. Tel: 09 357 8400. For InterCity Travel Centre, see **Coaches** on pages 186–7.

## SENIOR CITIZENS

There are few limitations for the senior citizen travelling in New Zealand; in fact, the Kiwis' innate sense of hospitality and general helpfulness means that you will probably find it an easier destination than many others. The main discounts are on the railways, where senior citizen fares offer a saving of around 30 per cent on standard tickets for those over 60 (proof of age required).

## STUDENT AND YOUTH TRAVEL

Being a young nation itself, New Zealand is well geared up to cater for the needs of student and youth travellers. A wide range of youth and student discounts on internal travel is available through the Student Travel Agency (STA), which has branches throughout the country; it also issues International Student Identity Cards. InterCity offers a range of discounts on rail, ferry and coach travel: a YHA Travel Card ($24) will give you up to 50 per cent off all services; and the VIP Backpacker Card ($25) consists of vouchers that give discounts on coach travel only. Mount Cook Landlines and Newmans offer similar deals for coach travel.

**STA International Travellers Centre**, 10 High Street, Auckland (tel: 09 309 0458).

**Youth Hostels Association**: 28 Worcester Street, PO Box 436 Christchurch and Australia House, 36 Customs Street East, Auckland. The *Youth Hostels Guide* contains a list of addresses, phone numbers and maps.

## TELEPHONES

The Telecom Corporation provides both national and international services and operates three types of payphones, colour-coded: card phone booths – green;
credit card booths – yellow;
coin operated booths – blue.

The majority of public telephones now use phonecards, which are available from newsagents, supermarkets, petrol stations and other retail outlets. There are also around 200 credit card telephones around the country.

You can make direct-dial international calls from most telephone-boxes; as elsewhere in the world, hotels and motels impose surcharges for international calls.

Travellers can obtain Telecom calling cards which charge the calls to your home telephone bill.

Young travellers and students can benefit from a wide range of discounts